5/31/12

Pauline,

Thank you for sharing the love of God with the people of Haiti. Through your service. May the Lord richly bless you.

Jesus is the Answer!

The Hidden Ruler of Haiti

The Root of Haiti's Socio-economic Problems

Dr. Pierre Rigaud Julien

Scriptures in this publication are taken from the New King James version of the Bible or paraphrased by the author.

The Hidden Ruler of Haiti
Third Edition

ISBN 13: 978-0-9796675-4-1
ISBN 10: 0-9796675-4-2

Copyright © 2008 by Pierre Rigaud Julien

All rights reserved. Contents and/or cover of this book may not be reproduced or transmitted in any form or by any means, electronically or mechanically, without written permission from the author and publisher.

To request written permission to reproduce sections of this publication, contact the author:

www.blessinghealing.org
or
EMAIL: admin@blessinghealing.org

Contents

Introduction—Letter to the Haitian People

Chapters

1. A Nation in Bondage **9**
- Haiti: A Historical Introduction
- A Continual Search for a Liberator
- A New Image

2. The Hidden Ruler of Haiti **13**
- Statement of the Problem
- Satan Is the Hidden Ruler of Haiti
- The Reality of the Invisible World
- The Voodoo Influence in Haiti
- The Reality of Living in Haiti

3. My Personal Testimony **21**
- Growing Up in Haiti
- The Cycle Continues
- My Conversion
- My Struggle with My Past
- My First Visit to Haiti after 16 Years
- The Creation of My Ministry
- May God Bless America!

4. What Will it Take to Heal Haiti? 47
- The United Nations Is Not the Solution
- A Haitian Leader with Good Intentions Is Not the Solution
- Haiti Can Be Healed!
- Spiritual Solution
- God Needs a "Nehemiah" for the Reconstruction of Haiti
- It Will Take Divine Intervention Through the Work of Faithful Christians
- The Message to the Haitian People: "Repent, Be Baptized, and Be Filled With the Holy Spirit!"

5. The Roadmap to Haiti's Deliverance .. 59
- Biblical Perspective
- The Book of Nehemiah – A Model for the Haitian People

6. The Reconstruction of Haiti 69
- May God Bless Haiti!
- Political & Socio-economic Solution
- National Political Process
- Five Years Reconstruction Objectives

7. A Love Letter from God 83
- Message of the Cross
- The Power of the Gospel

Introduction

If My people who are called by My name will humble themselves, and pray and seek My face and turn from their wicked ways, then I will hear from heaven, and will forgive their sin and heal their land. (2 Chronicles 7:14)

To the People of Haiti:

Greetings in the Name of the Lord Jesus Christ.

My dear Haitian brothers and sisters, this book is dedicated to you. Praise be to God who inspires me to share with you some fundamental truths and spiritual insights that will change your lives and heal our nation. I write this book in love and not to criticize anyone but rather to give you hope. Reading this book may spark deep emotions and strong reactions. However, I encourage you to read it entirely with an open mind, and reflect on the truth I am sharing with you.

First, I want you to know how profoundly my heart grieves to see the affliction of our people. It hurts me deeply to see our country in abject poverty. In spite of considerable amount of economic assistance and various forms of intervention to create sustainable hope and prosperity for our people, Haiti remains unable to escape poverty, insecurity, and a host of other interrelated problems. After 200 years of sovereignty, our nation continues to be known for its history of political instability, poverty, and desolation.

Introduction

This book recommends a new course of action to solve Haiti's socio-economic problems and challenges any interested individual to consider the spiritual deficiencies embedded in the Haitian culture. The practices of voodoo, adultery, fornication, and idolatry are undeniably sinful and detestable in the sight of God and constitute a hindrance to national prosperity. Sin is the dominant national problem. The violation of God's principles creates a breakdown of natural order, leading to spiritual emptiness and physical harm to our society. For the wages of sin is death, but the gift of God is eternal life through Jesus Christ our Lord (Romans 6:23). No individual or nation can escape the judgment that is embedded in sinful behavior. The solution to Haiti's socio-economic problems is relatively simple, but the world rejects it. The solution is achievable, but it is disregarded. It is the only answer, but the Haitian people continue to ignore it. Jesus Christ is the only answer, and national repentance is the first step to the healing process of the nation.

I am inviting you to join with me in prayer and fasting for our beloved country, while seeking a new approach for a better life in Christ Jesus for our people and for our nation. Will you humble yourselves with me, pray, seek God's face, and turn from all wickedness to allow God to hear our prayers, forgive our sins, and heal our land? By faith, I believe you have accepted this invitation. Therefore, in the name of the Lord Jesus Christ, we can already begin to proclaim together the healing and deliverance of our nation from all generational curses!

JESUS IS THE ANSWER!

Your brother in Christ,

Pierre Rigaud Julien

Chapter 1

A Nation in Bondage

Surely the arm of the LORD is not too short to save, nor his ear too dull to hear. But your iniquities have separated you from your God; your sins have hidden his face from you, so that he will not hear. For your hands are stained with blood, your fingers with guilt. Your lips have spoken lies, and your tongue mutters wicked things. No-one calls for justice; no-one pleads his case with integrity. They rely on empty arguments and speak lies; they conceive trouble and give birth to evil. (Isaiah 59:1-4)

Haiti – A Historical Introduction

Christopher Columbus discovered the island of Hispaniola in 1492. The Taino Indians who inhabited the island were virtually annihilated by Spanish settlers within 25 years. In the early 17th century, the French established a presence on Hispaniola, and in 1697, Spain ceded the western part of the island to France, which later became Haiti. The French colony became one of the wealthiest in the Caribbean due to forestry, sugar industries, and the importation of African slaves. At the end of the 18th century, nearly five hundred thousand Haitian slaves revolted under the leadership of Toussaint Louverture. In 1804, after a long struggle, Haiti became the first independent black republic in the world.

Throughout Haiti's history, political instability, voodoo, and poverty have been constant and common factors in the lives of the Haitian people. From self-appointed leaders, foreign occupation, military coups, dictatorial regimes, and elected leaders, the Haitian people remain distressed in their search for better living conditions. In February 2004, elected President Jean-Bertrand Aristide was forced to leave the country, and an interim government was appointed to organize new elections under the auspices of the United Nations Stabilization Mission in Haiti. In May 2006, after a period of violence and irregularities in the elections, the Haitian people elected President René Préval.

Haiti has an estimated population of 8,924,553 inhabitants with a median age of 18 years and literacy rate of fifty-three percent. Eighty percent of the Haitian population lives in poverty. Two-thirds of all Haitians do not have formal jobs but depend on the agricultural sector, mainly small-scale subsistence farming. Their crops remain vulnerable to damage caused by frequent natural disasters, including floods that are exacerbated by the country's widespread deforestation. The government relies on international economic assistance for fiscal sustainability. Haiti is ninety six percent Christians (including Catholic and Protestant) and four percent other denominations. However, roughly more than half of the population believes or practices some form of voodoo. (1)

A Continual Search for a Liberator

200 years after its creation, the first independent black republic in the world is now one of the poorest countries of the northern hemisphere. While the Haitian people should have been glorifying God for their independ-

ence, they fervently honored Satan instead through voodoo worship. The majority of Haitians today continue to give credit to Satan for this victory, believing that their ancestors obtained supernatural favors and protection through the practice of voodoo resulting in their national independence. However, the Haitian people have never actually enjoyed true freedom and independence. Extreme poverty resulting from corruption and other sinful practices keep them in bondage. The majority believe in voodoo and reject the love of God by putting their faith in demonic spirits, known as "loa." The need for spiritual revival in Haiti is vital. The renewal of the Haitian people's minds, beliefs, and values must be the focus of any effort to affect positive and lasting change in the social structure and degrading national living conditions.

A New Image

It is time to change the negative image of Haiti. For some, Haiti projects the image of a wasteland inhabited by selfish thugs, a cursed nation where voodoo is the central factor affecting people's lives, and a destitute country where corruption is primarily the standard. For many others, Haiti reflects a country plagued by criminals, kidnappers who murder men, women, and children for money. Still others view Haiti as a nation detested by its own people, where nobody can be trusted, and a people buried in the darkness of sin, fleeing their own country by boat in search of a better life away from their homeland.

The truth is that Haitians are hardworking, ingenious, and warmhearted people. Sadly, like a flock of sheep lost in a desert without a shepherd to care for them, the Haitian people are in urgent need of unconditional love. The people need to find someone to trust and lead them in righteousness and the fear of God.

They are seeking, yet they cannot find because they do not know exactly what they need, for whom to look, and where to find him. Consequently, they find themselves entangled in a cycle of poverty and despair in search of a liberator. The Haitian people become vulnerable to abuse, discrimination, and rejection around the world, even by Haiti's closest friends and neighbors. Haiti has lost its sense of purpose and many of its people have become unwanted refugees around the world.

Haiti's problems are deep and complex, requiring drastic changes. Haitians can no longer delay the process of change. A new approach to Haiti's socio-economic problems is urgent if the nation is to be healed and restored to its rightful dignity. The process must begin with the change of Haiti's image and identity. Indeed, Haiti needs a new identity: A Christian Republic, a nation built on biblical principles, and with the indwelling of the Spirit of Christ in the hearts of the Haitian people.

Chapter 2

The Hidden Ruler of Haiti:

The Root of Haiti's Socio-economic Problems

The thief comes only to steal and kill and destroy; I have come that they may have life, and have it to the full. (John 10:10)

Statement of the Problem

The socio-economic problems addressed in this book relate to differing perceptions of the root cause of poverty in Haiti. Inefficiency in public sector administration, decaying moral and cultural beliefs, lack of investment in human and physical infrastructure, and inadequate educational opportunities all have had very adverse impacts on Haiti's economy and family dynamics. However, after carefully considering Haiti's history and traditions and assessing the trends of the nation's socio-economic difficulties, I am convinced that "satanic influence" is the root cause of the problems facing the Haitian people.

Despite their good intentions, the Haitian people live in a state of "continual breakdown." In general, some of the national traditions and core values such as adultery, fornication, idolatry, and voodoo worship attract satanic activities and naturally lead to poverty.

This truth is self-evident. It is traditionally accepted for a man to be legally married and simultaneously maintain one or more other conjugal relations. Often, the women involved in these relationships become friends. I was born into this type of relationship. It is also a widespread practice in Haiti for a man and woman to live together for many years, have children, and call themselves husband and wife without ever getting married. Many of these children born out of wedlock grow up without strong parental guidance and in an environment of sinful practices and, therefore, continue the cycle of fornication and adultery.

Worshiping of the dead is also a common practice in Haiti. In Haitian customs, the dead are still valuable resources. People continue to visit the tomb with candles to worship, pray, and ask deceased relatives for protection and dreams that would lead to winning lottery numbers and other favors. These sinful behaviors widely accepted and integrated into the national culture inhibit progress of the economic system and quality of life. Clearly, immoral and sinful practices have negative consequences and perpetuate behavior that is counterproductive to positive outcomes. They also violate divine principles for a prosperous life and ultimately lead to the wrath of God.

The United Nations (UN) and the Haitian government continue to misdiagnose Haiti's problems. Consequently, their prescriptions to solve the problems have been ineffective. Haiti is currently experiencing a spiritual problem that engenders the nation's socio-economic dilemma. Unless this spiritual problem is recognized and dealt with attentively as a matter of great national priority, Haiti cannot prosper. The war for the deliverance of Haiti is not against human beings but against wicked demonic spirits in control of the nation with legal authority.

Haiti's problems can be attributed to the voodoo foundation on which the nation was built. Satan comes to kill, steal and destroy (John 10:10). Consequently, demonic influences have been the main source of all evils in the country. Throughout Haiti's history, it has been the case that even the leaders with good intentions in the beginning have failed to have a lasting positive impact because Satan succeeded in filling their hearts with selfish motives. Once tempted with the love of fame, power, and money, any Haitian political or religious leader will fail unless his or her primary motive is to reconcile the nation to God through repentance and faith in Jesus Christ, humbly serve and lead the Haitian people to prosperity.

Satan is the Hidden Ruler of Haiti

Satan's invisible hands are actively at work in Haiti, influencing every aspect of national life. A nominee for public office in Haiti must realize above all things that Satan is already sitting on the chairs in all government offices. Satan is ready to inspire dishonest ideas, temptations to do evil, and to perpetuate corruption. It is his nature to inspire only deceitful thoughts. Without the Holy Spirit's presence and control in our lives, it is very difficult to resist and overcome Satan's temptations. For this reason, God promises never to allow Christians to be tempted beyond their abilities to overcome the temptation. This promise is strictly for those who are in Christ and who want to live a life pleasing to God.

"No temptation has overtaken you except such as is common to man; but God is faithful, who will not allow you to be tempted beyond what you are able, but with the temptation will also make the way of escape, that you may be able to bear it" (1 Corinthians 10:13).

Two leading contemporary Haitian leaders, President Aristide and Prime Minister Latortue, had unprecedented opportunities to make a significant difference in the lives of the Haitian people and the reconstruction of the nation. Aristide was a simple Catholic priest who demonstrated genuine concern for the cause of the underprivileged Haitian people. He was a friend of the poor and an advocate for their causes. In contrast, Latortue lived a life of privilege in the United States. He was as an honest critic of political leaders in Haiti through radio and television programs. He claimed to have the answers to the problems in Haiti. He was given the opportunity to return to Haiti to provide his contribution in solving the nation's socio-economic problems. Both Aristide and Latortue became Chief Executives of the nation. In considering their performance in fulfilling their service to the nation, we easily see the fruit of their labor: the socio-economic conditions have gotten significantly worse, and insecurity and violence have increased as never before in the history of the nation.

I am certain that these two leaders had **good intentions** for the development and prosperity of Haiti. But they did not succeed because they lacked divine resources to overcome Satan's temptations. Their primary motive was not to glorify the Almighty God.

The Reality of the Invisible World

We must not ignore or underestimate the influence of the spiritual world over our physical existence. God, who is invisible, creates the physical world; He lives in the invisible world. Therefore, it is important to underline the impact in the spiritual realm of the decisions made by a Head of State upon the people he or she is governing. When the Haitian ancestors and a president of the Republic committed the nation to demonic forces through voodoo worship, Satan was thus granted legal authority to subdue the people and keep them in bondage.

In the Bible, Adam was given authority over all of God's creation. Adam's disobedience to God causes sin to enter the world, which gives legal authority to Satan to keep people in the bondage of sin. Likewise, knowing that Jesus is the answer to the problem of sin, Satan tempted Him to disobey God by offering Him the kingdoms of the world and their glory only if Jesus would worship him. In response, Jesus quoted the Scriptures: *"You shall worship the Lord your God and Him only you shall serve" (Matthew 4:9-10)*. Jesus, by his faithfulness to God, becomes the only way to freedom from Satan's bondage.

Similarly, it will take a faithful Haitian Head of State to lead the people to national repentance and faith in Jesus Christ, commit the nation to God, dethrone Satan and remove his stronghold in Haiti.

There is biblical support to this statement. The Bible gives an account of King David in 1 Chronicles 21:1-17 where Satan influenced David to conduct a census of the population of Israel. God was displeased with David's action and struck the Jewish people by sending a plague on the nation. The Scripture says 70,000 men of Israel fell dead. David responds to God by saying: "Is it not I who commanded to count the enumeration the people? Indeed I am the one who has sinned and done wickedly, but these sheep what have they done? O Lord my God, please let your hand be against me and my father's household but not against your people that they should be plagued." David repented of his sin against God, but his nation suffered the enormous consequences of its leader's sin.

The Voodoo Influence in Haiti

As already indicated, an important aspect of Haiti's history and cultural values are deeply rooted in voodoo. Former president Jean Bertrand Aristide officially certified voodoo as a religion in 2003, allowing practitioners to perform religious ceremonies with legal authority.(2)

Voodoo practitioners normally offer sacrifices such as animal blood, food, dance, and alcohol in their supplications to demonic spirits called "Loa." In many communities around the country where there are no adequate medical facilities, a voodoo priest may be the primary health care provider. His services range from childbirth to prescription of holistic medicine for sickness and diseases. Many Haitians, including my parents, see no conflict in practicing voodoo, while adhering to their Christian faith. I grew up in that environment.

The Reality of Living in Haiti

The majority of Haitians work in agriculture, mostly as small subsistence farmers. Agricultural production suffers from the effects of severe deforestation, land erosion, primitive farming techniques, and lack of public and private investment. It is shocking that the majority of Haitian farmers still use machetes, hacks, and shovels as their primary means to prepare and cultivate the land. Almost all foreign investment companies have left the country because of insecurity and poor infrastructure. Most of the products and items sold in the Haitian market are imported.

Haiti has two major ports located in Port-au-Prince and Cap-Haitian and twelve minor ports. Most port facilities are in poor conditions, and port fees are extremely high. Like the ports, the roads are mostly unpaved and in very poor conditions. The majority of the Haitian population have no access to electricity and drinking water in their homes. The interruption of services is very common in places even where these services are offered to the residents. The problem of deforestation is enormous throughout the country. The majority of the population use wood as the primary energy method for the preparation of food. In addition, high population growth and lack of economic opportunities provoke urban migration. Accordingly, the living conditions of the poor continue to deteriorate dramatically. Increased social and political tensions have contributed to a vicious cycle of increased vulnerability, degradation of social, spiritual, economic, and environmental resources. The sanitary conditions are deplorable in Haiti. Poor living conditions compounded by the lack of proper drinking water and sanitation continue to add to health problems at the national level.

The national education system in Haiti, like other sectors of national life, reflects the unbearable struggle with poverty that most Haitians encounter. Public education is free but widely unavailable. Private schools accounts for about 75% of all educational programs. Although Haitians place a high value on education, many families cannot afford the fees required to educate their children.(3)

Chapter 3

My Personal Testimony

For God so loved the world that he gave his one and only Son, that whoever believes in him shall not perish but have eternal life. (John 3:16)

Growing Up in Haiti

I was born out of wedlock. My mother was married to the father of four of my half brothers. Her husband had nine other children from other conjugal relationships while he was married to my mother. My mother separated from her husband and entered into conjugal relationship with my father. My father was already married and also had seven children with his wife. My father never separated from his wife but was fully permitted to enter in a conjugal relationship with my mother. In fact my mother and my father's wife had a cordial relationship. From my parents' extra-marital affair, my sister Ryonne and I were born. Unfortunately, Ryonne died at the age of two. My father informed me that someone killed her out of jealousy by using a voodoo spell.

My father's wife is alive today at the age of 96. She is healthy and at peace with God. She has always displayed sincere love and affection for me. My brothers on both sides have never considered me inferior. They treated me so well, I never knew that I was "different" because of my status as an illegitimate child. I did not realize until I was much older that I did not really have a "full" sibling. During my father's extra-marital affair with my mother, he got involved in a third conjugal relationship with another woman. From this relationship, another child was born. Again, both my mother and my father's wife had a good relationship with this woman. Sadly, the example of my parents is the norm in Haitian society even today.

My Childhood

I had a happy, protected, active, and fulfilled childhood. I had many good friends of whom I keep excellent memories. Even today, memories of my childhood still give me indescribable joy. I often went hunting all day with some of my friends. We also played "Flag," a very fun sport. Soccer was my favorite sport. Swimming in the Grand' Anse river was a casual daily activity for us. My friend Arsene actually saved me from drowning while I was swimming in a deep area of the river. I also enjoyed riding horses. In fact, I had my own horse. Often my father would allow me to accompany him on horseback to our farms in Dicongé. I enjoyed watching voodoo ceremonies. Very often, my parents held voodoo dances and offered food to the spirit they worshiped.

The most influential people in my life were my father and mother. Despite the negative values I learned from my parents because of their deeply rooted cultural beliefs, they also taught me the values of hard work, respect for authority, community service, and love for my neighbors. Another influential person in my life was one of my elementary school teachers, Mr. Dominique, also known as Professor Dodo. He was my teacher for two years. I had great respect for him because he truly cared for his students. There was a woman named Rose in my community who also had a great impact on my life. One day as I was returning from school in Moron, an adjoining city about 90 minutes of walking distance from my hometown, she overheard me using an offensive word and corrected me on the spot. Consequently, she escorted me home to report me to my parents for my derogatory conduct in the street. I appreciate her intervention to this very day, and I still maintain contact with her in Haiti after more than thirty years. Later in my life, one of my brothers had the most and lasting impact on my life. I owe him beyond measure for my success in life. He became my provider and ensured I lacked nothing. I thank God for him!

Truly, God who created me and knew me before the foundation of the world had a set plan and an appointed course for my life. I believe that if it had not been for God, I would be dead or near death today. He has protected me supernaturally in ways that I can never attempt to explain. While living in Florida at age 18, two women with whom I had sexual intercourse were diagnosed with AIDS during the time I was sexually active with them. They were also close family friends and have all died as a result of AIDS. One of them knew she had AIDS but ensured my protection through prophylactics during intercourse. The other one was well respected by my relatives and may not have known that she was HIV positive. Jesus rescued me from death and my sinful ways and now calls me to bring light to my people in Haiti. Praise and glory be to my Lord and Savior Jesus Christ. How merciful and gracious He is indeed!

I know firsthand the magnitude of the problems in Haiti. Satan has successfully blinded the minds of many Haitian so that they remain in darkness and ungodly living conditions leading them to poverty and despair. Until Jesus saved me, I could not see how far I was traveling in darkness, lost and without God in this world. Sometimes a quick thought of my past foolish actions hurt my heart deeply. I just thank God—He removed me from darkness into His marvelous light. Glory be to His Name forever!

My Father - Dacy Daphnis

I was born in my father's old age. He was a well-respected member of the community. He held various public offices in the community. He was a judge (Justice of the Peace) and retired as the Registrar of birth and death. He was also a farmer. I still have a vivid memory of my father. He was a caring man. He was always available and willing to advise and assist the people in surrounding villages even after his retirement. He helped the people when others falsely accused them. After examining their cases, he would compassionately stand up for them as a character witness. He usually had me handwrite letters of support for the accused to other officials in the justice system while he dictated the contents to me.

He was a loving father. I have many treasured memories of spending time with him. I remember how he read to me at night. He normally sat me on his lap to read his favorite story from an old Haitian school reading textbook known as "Lecture Courante." His favorite story was "Le laboureur et ses enfants" (The laborer and His children). Before the laborer died, he called his children together and informed them that great treasures were hidden in the land. They would find the hidden treasures only if they dug and cultivated the land. He used this story to instill in me the importance of hard work.

My father was a great farmer. He enjoyed riding his horses to attend his farms in Dicongé, which is approximately two hours in the mountains from our home. During harvest time, and when school was closed, he would take the family there for a few days to sow or reap depending on the season. I enjoyed the season of harvesting cocoa. We collected raw cocoa beans from the tree, transported the product home, and prepared it for selling at the market. That was a privilege because cocoa is one of the major crops that Haiti produces and exports. Therefore, it was a great opportunity for us to earn some money.

My father had many servants. Normally in the Haitian society, the servants live in the house and are an integral part of the family. My father also had gardeners who tended to the land and helped with the various aspects of farming.

My father was also a man of prayer. He habitually spoke blessings upon his children: "I have five sons – five millionaires." He had a great vision for us. In his house he built a room solely devoted to prayer. It was customary for him to pray daily. He had various books of prayers. His favorite was titled, "L'ange Conducteur." Like most Haitians, my father practiced the Roman Catholic faith. However, he was an even stronger voodoo practitioner. He told us stories of the spirit he personally called upon for supernatural favors and protection. He was once in route towards Les Cayes, another city about two full days of travel on horseback from our hometown. While crossing a river, he was struck by an inexplicable force that caused him to fall in the water. He got out of the water under the influence of the spirit with a stone in his hand. He considered the stone as a symbol of the spirit or loa he has received. In the Haitian custom, each "Loa" has a name and is known to the practitioner by the revealed name. Maitre Ignace (Master Ignace) was the "Family Loa" that my father worshiped. He normally called upon the name of Ignace when praying for the protection of his family. He always had a special lamp, a candle, a small bell and a glass of water present to begin his intercessory prayers to the Loa. Sometimes people came to him for prayers to cast out demonic spirit that caused physical infirmities and other types of afflictions. In those cases, the afflicted person would undergo 7, 14, or 21 days in our house for a period of intense prayers and fasting by sleeping on a floor mat. My father normally led the evening prayers. The afflicted person was normally healed at the end of the appointed time of prayers.

My father had strong faith in the demonic spirit to satisfy any needs for healing and protection. Several times a year my father offered food to the spirit, a ceremony known as "manjé lezanj or manjé marasa." Once a year, my father would also conduct a voodoo ceremony with a dance known as "bal bourette" to honor his Loa.

My father usually called on me to read from the prayer book at night. He was passing his belief on to me, which he did successfully. One night during prayer, he was filled with a supernatural spirit while calling upon Maitre Ignace. However, on that night I saw my father filled with a spirit who identified himself as "Maitre Ignace." The spirit spoke through my father and prophesied the return of my oldest brother who was living in New York at the time. The spirit said that my brother would return to Haiti to accept a position in the Haitian government. The spirit said that this was the beginning of the work that he was preparing for my brother. Within a few weeks of this revelation, my brother was offered and accepted a position in Haiti.

Many Haitians seek favors from the Loa to obtain jobs. It is customary for Haitians to visit a voodoo priest after having a dream. It is expected of the voodoo priest to inform the visitor of the purpose of the visit. The test of a true voodoo priest is his ability to accurately tell the visitor the reason for his or her visit without any help from the visitor.

As a child, there was also an aspect of my father's life I did not like. Since Thursday was flea market day in our community, people from surrounding communities throughout the state would come to trade in our community. My father usually returned home drunk every Thursday after the flea market. I never saw him drink alcohol in the home. In fact, I believe this was the only day of the week he drank alcoholic beverages. My mother was a merchant commonly known in Haiti as "Madan sara." She spent the day trading and selling her goods in the market. It was always heartbreaking to watch her deal with my father on Thursdays after the market since he would return home inebriated. He used profanity loudly and publicly cursed out my mother for no reason. It always disturbed me how his personality changed so drastically on Thursdays after drinking excessive alcohol. This was an amazing phenomenon to me because other respected men in the community would also get filthy drunk on Thursday at the market place. Like my father, they too acted out of character as a result of their drunkenness. This degrading ritual was expected from them every Thursday after a day of trading in the market place.

In spite of how my father helped others who were ill, it did not make him immune to illness. I was about 10 years old when my father became deathly ill. It was so serious that the family made preparations for his burial. A voodoo priest came from another state to care for him and restore him back to health. After several months of intervention, my father made a complete recovery and lived many years after that experience. As a result, he stopped drinking completely. During that terrible experience I was able to see how much the people from surrounding communities truly respected and honored him. During the time of his affliction, the house was constantly full with well wishers who came to provide support and to help in any way necessary. It is traditionally a Haitian custom for well-wishers to come and stay at the afflicted person's house for many days to provide assistance as needed. The voodoo priest stayed with our family throughout the entire period of my father's illness and many months thereafter. My father died in 1986. By that time, I was already serving in the United States Army and stationed in Germany. My deepest sorrow to this day is that I do not believe that my father ever confessed and accepted Jesus Christ as his personal Lord and Savior.

My Mother - Anne Clemande Julien

She was a small lady in stature and full of energy. She had great acumen for business and entrepreneurial endeavors. She was a retailer and wholesaler of various products. She sold clothing and various other articles in the market and traded corn and tobacco wholesale. She filled up large transport cargo trucks with goods that were taken to the port in Jérémie, our state's biggest city, to be loaded onto a ship. The goods were transported to larger markets in Port-au-Prince, our capital. She often traveled to Port-au-Prince on business trips to purchase goods and receive her proceeds from agents, normally other brokers who sold her goods to exporters and various other retailers. According to our community standards, my parents were considered wealthy.

My mother was a hard working and respected woman in the community. Although she had excellent business sense and good accounting skills, she did not learn how to read and write until she was an older adult. She became so excited about reading and writing that she bought a piece of land adjoining her house and built a community center for illiterate adults. She hired a teacher and provided free writing and reading lessons to any adult in the community who desired to learn how to read and write. After her death, the school unfortunately fell into a state of despair. Later, my brother Reverend Jean Ridly Julien improved the school and founded "Anne Clemande Julien Foundation" in honor of our mother. Today, the foundation provides free education to orphans and poor children. In keeping with our mother's vision, the Foundation also provides free technical skill opportunities to adults. Currently, there are more than 300 children and more than 50 adults enrolled in the school. The foundation currently provides employment opportunities to twelve people in the village.

My mother was an ideal friend and neighbor. She had many close friends. My mother and two of our neighbors, Marie and Mrs. Denis, exchanged a plate of food everyday with each other. That routine was expected every day. They had great harmony, respect, and love for each other. They were always available to help each other in times of need. Unfortunately, this sense of friendship and community outreach is disappearing in Haiti because of the increasing crime rate, lack of trust resulting from hopelessness. Today in Haiti finding trustworthy individuals is exceptionally rare, especially when money is a factor.

My mother was a devout Catholic. At that time, the Catholic Church conducted Mass in Latin. Often, returning home from church, she continued to sing hymns in Latin, although she did not understand what was really said. On the other hand, just like my father and countless other Haitian families, she was also a profound practitioner of voodoo. Once, a burglary occurred in her home while we were away for a few days. The thieves had stolen money and other valuable articles. This was very uncommon since the community was small, and we all knew each other. We had one well-known thief in the community. Normally, when something was stolen, by default, he was the number one suspect. However, my mother sent someone to consult a voodoo priest. The messenger returned with the identification of the two men who committed the robbery and with a recommended voodoo ritual that could be used against them.

Both my parents thought in their hearts that they loved God and were serving God. I truly believe that they did not see any offense against God by their voodoo practices and adulterous lifestyle.

My Community

I was born in Chambellan, a small village with a population of about 35,000 people today. When I lived in Chambellan, there was only one public school but my parents chose to send me and my siblings to another public school located in an adjoining city. Throughout my seven years of elementary education, I walked at least 90 minutes one way to school Monday to Friday. I had to get up early, but I became accustomed to it and enjoyed the daily walk back and forth to school. This was also a great time to play with my friends.

My immediate neighbors were Louis, Sile, Mrs. Denis, Tinaud, Beloth, and Marie. The first three: Louis, Sile and Mrs. Denis were voodoo priests and priestess, also known as Houngan or Bocor and Mambo. One of my paternal uncles was a voodoo priest. He died early, and I did not get to know him. Everyone in the community was impacted in some way by the effect of voodoo. There were many Protestants in the community. In fact, there was a large Baptist church maybe two miles from my home. This church is still functioning today. I do not have any childhood memories of any significant efforts to conduct Christian spiritual revivals in the community.

The whole village was involved in the life of each child in the village. It was customary for adults to tell stories at night and also for young people to share what is called "conte," or storytelling. It was always fun when children from the surroundings would meet in my father's house to share "conte" and tell "folk stories." In telling a conte, a person would give the outcome of an event, and the audience would then be challenged to guess the event. Other forms of conte can be the description of an object followed by the challenge for the audience to guess the name of the object. Our family friend Tidé sometimes played the guitar and sang traditional songs. My father sometimes told stories regarding the work of the devil. He told these stories not to scare us but to educate us.

We had no electricity. At about 8 PM when darkness was setting in, most families retired for the evening. We were told that the devil works at night. Unless there was an emergency, most people did not leave their homes after 10 PM. It is widely believed in Haiti that people can be transformed into dogs at night as they practice demonic rituals. My parents certainly believed this, and my father said he had had personal encounters with dogs during the night that were actually people he knew. He told us that one night, a dog approached him on the road and walked around him. The following day a friend told him about the encounter and advised him not to walk too late at night. My father thought that this person was the dog he met.

Like most Haitians, my father believed that people used voodoo spells to kill others or to make them sick. He believed that people who had been killed through voodoo spells could be raised from the dead and turned into a cow to be sold at the market place. It is also widely believed that a person can be transformed into a horse and be used in this way during the night.

I share these stories to illustrate to the readers the depth of this belief in Haiti. Throughout my childhood, I believed these stories were fact and not fiction. Unfortunately, many Haitians still maintain these evil traditions that will continue to keep them in darkness, and the bondage of sin and poverty. Consequently, since these people do not know God, they spend a lot of time trying to appease these demonic spirits by serving and worshiping them through voodoo ceremonies.

The Cycle Continues

My brothers followed into my father's footsteps in voodoo and adultery. Although the eldest brother seemed to have been hit the hardest by our father's example, we all are guilty of the sins of our fathers. The oldest of my brothers is married and has 14 children from seven different women. He continued the voodoo practices of our father. Fortunately, he finally came to the knowledge of God's love and accepted Jesus Christ as his personal Savior. He is now a Deacon in a Seventh Day Adventist Church. The second oldest brother also married, is blessed with four children, all of whom are well established. However, he also has a son born to him outside of his marriage. He became a fervent voodoo practitioner as well. The third oldest brother became a Seventh Day Adventist early in life and broke the cycle of voodoo practices and adultery. He has been a Seventh Day Adventist pastor in Haiti for over 28 years. With the exception of the brother who received Jesus Christ as his Lord and Savior early in life, we all became voodoo practitioners and were unfaithful in our marital relationships. To us, having extra-marital relationships were simply an acceptable way of life in our culture. We did not find it disrespectful or sinful.

My brothers from my mother's side followed a similar pattern. The eldest one has four illegitimate children by three different women. The second oldest brother has a daughter out of wedlock. Nonetheless, the third brother is a Catholic priest. He also broke the cycle. He and I are working together through Anne Clémande Julien Foundation in Chambellan to make a difference in our village to the glory of God.

My life was similar to my father and my brothers. In fact, when I first met my wife Carolyn, I told her that I must have a "mistress" in addition to my wife. She did not take my statement seriously; she thought I was joking. After we were married, she discovered that my statement was not a joke. This caused many problems in our relationship.

My Conversion

I met my wife Carolyn in September 1989. She is a Christian and actively involved in church activities. For almost 10 years members of her church prayed for me. I didn't like to go there because the pastor, Hattie Lathan, often called me up to pray for me. One time, a visiting pastor called me out and asked me to run around the church. I was infuriated, but I obeyed him because I didn't want to embarrass Carolyn. I developed a technique of starting an argument with her on Saturday night so that she would not ask me to attend church with her on Sunday morning. That technique worked for a while until one Sunday morning our eight-year-old son came into my room and pulled the sheet off me and said, "Get up and go to church with your family!" His words profoundly touched me. Two weeks before my conversion, one of the ministers, Pastor Rosa Jackson, told Carolyn, "The Lord is about to knock him down and it will happen very soon." I laughed at her statement.

I was saved on January 2, 2003, while stationed at Fort Lee, Virginia. My conversion happened while watching a television program with Pat Robertson on the Christian Broadcasting Network (CBN). I saw two men on the program giving testimonies regarding how Jesus changed their lives. One of the men was a Jew who served in the Israeli army. The other was a Palestinian who used to conduct aggressive acts against the Israeli. Both men came to the US and became Christians. I saw that something had happened in their lives that caused radical changes in them. As I heard how Jesus changed their lives, I was profoundly moved by their testimonies that I wanted to be changed also.

Nevertheless, when I saw this fervent testimony on CBN, I made up my mind that I wanted to be a faithful and committed Christian. I prayed this simple prayer to God:

"Lord Jesus, I receive you now as my Savior. Please forgive me of my sins. I've made up my mind to do your will; I don't want to be a "Sunday Morning" Christian. I want your power to flow in me as I trust you with my life - Amen!"

Immediately, I called my wife and my son Joshua and informed them that I accepted Jesus as my Lord and Savior. I asked them to accompany me to a Christian bookstore to purchase my Bible. We all rejoiced! I also purchased another book by Tim Layhe entitled, *How to Study the Bible for Yourself.* As I read this book, I came across this line, "No Bible reading, no breakfast." I embraced this idea and made my commitment to God that I would not eat natural food until after I had fed my spirit with the word of God. I have stuck to this commitment without ceasing since the day I made the vow.

I was determined to have praise and worship time with my family every evening at 9 PM. This ritual has become our family tradition. The family meets every evening to pray and conduct a Bible study. One night, ten days after I was saved, I went to bed after praying and praising God. While I was in my bed meditating, I saw a cluster of bright stars that are joined together to form a small rotating circle on my wall for at least 45 seconds. I quickly got out my bed and knelt down to thank God for visiting me. On this particular night, I slept in the guest room because I could not sleep well during the first few weeks of my conversion. I fought bad dreams that caused me to wake up several times during the night to pray and read the Bible. After seeing the stars on my wall, I got up to share the news with my wife, and we both began to praise God again. That night, as I was singing and praising God, the Lord filled me with the Holy Spirit, evidenced by speaking in new tongues as the Holy Spirit gave me utterance. We kept praising God for a long time, and then I returned to bed. Again that same night, the Lord spoke to me and said, "I give you the gift of healing."

The following night, I prayed and asked God to reveal His purpose for my life. Since He deemed me in right standing with Him to fill me with His Holy Spirit, then He must have a specific purpose for my life. Therefore, I desired to know what He had created me to accomplish for His kingdom. That evening God answered my prayer. In a dream, I was in Chambellan, my hometown, and I was on a stage preaching to a multitude of people on an open field. The next night I prayed again asking God for more instruction about this vision of preaching His gospel. It was never a part of my plan to be a preacher; never had the thought of preaching entered my mind. I asked this specific question: "Do I go to Chambellan after my retirement from the Army and build a church there to preach to the people?" The Lord answered me that night in the following manner. In a dream, I was in a classroom with other students. The teacher drew a map of Haiti and called my name out and pointed at the map and said, "Pierre Julien, this is your area of responsibility."

The following weekend, I returned to Fayetteville, North Carolina. The Bishop, Jobe Lathan, called me out during the Sunday morning service to inform me that the Lord spoke to him and told him to ordain me as a Minister of the Gospel of Jesus Christ. He further said to me, "I am going to ordain you out of obedience to God." He directed me to come on Saturdays to Fayetteville, North Carolina from Fort Lee, Virginia so that he could study one-on-one with me. He further recommended that I enroll in seminary or a college-level Bible study program.

His wife, Pastor Hattie Lathan, recommended that I visit a church in Virginia Beach, Virginia where a close friend of hers was a member. The following Sunday my family and I visited that church in Virginia Beach. At the end of the service, the pastor called my family and asked permission to pray for us. As he began to pray for us, he told me exactly everything that the Lord has revealed to me in the dreams. He told me that the Lord had given me the gift of healing and called me to preach. He said that the anointing of God will be manifested in my life with great power and miracles and that the Lord will establish me and my family in offices we never thought we would set foot. This prophecy confirmed other factors the Lord has revealed to me about His purpose for my life. In July 2003, Bishop Lathan fulfilled the command he believed he received from God and ordained me as a Minister of the Gospel of Jesus Christ. I preached that Sunday, and God performed great signs in the church, healing many who were sick including the Bishop's wife.

I never saw myself as a preacher. Although my heart was always filled with the desire to return to Haiti at some point and serve the Haitian people, but I never thought that it would be as a minister of the Word of God. Truly, before the foundation of the world, God knew me and had a plan for my life. On July 21, 2008, I returned to Haiti to begin my full-time ministry to the Haitian people.

My Struggle With My Past

From the day that Jesus opened my heart to believe in Him, I made up my mind to walk upright before the Lord and to honor Him all the days of my life. My spirit was instantly saved, but my mind was a war zone during the first 15 days after my conversion. Satan was bringing to my recollection my past sexual activities and voodoo experiences. I was having problems making love to my wife. Almost every night, I was having dreams of sexual activities with other women. I used to wake up crying because I thought I was sinning against God by having those dreams. Sometimes, while having sexual intercourse with my wife, I was physically with her but in my mind, I was with another woman. I was very disturbed because I did not understand what was going on. I tried with all my heart to resist those desires, but they kept returning with an even greater intensity. One day, I felt that my head was about to explode as I attempted to resist those sinful memories. The pressure was very heavy on my mind as I tried to resist those thoughts, and I began to cry. I got on my knees and called my wife and my son to lay hands on me and pray for me to overcome these thoughts. I told them what the problem was as I was crying on my knees. After their prayer, I felt a peace of mind I have never experienced before. That evening, as I was having sexual intercourse with my wife, the same old thoughts of other women began to penetrate my mind, and instantly I saw a hand that appeared and physically blocked the thought from entering my mind. Jesus delivered me that night from this perverse spirit. I got up and knelt down giving thanks to God for delivering me from this tormenting spirit. I knew without a doubt that Jesus delivered me that night!

Soon after this deliverance, I was battling lust of the eye, and the Holy Spirit told me, "Don't look at sin." This revelation has set me free from lust of the eyes. Every time a woman would pass by me, when the thought of looking tried to enter my mind, I hear the word "Don't look at sin" and I am able to resist the desire and overcome the thought. Jesus has set me free! Ultimately, intimacy with my wife is now better than I thought imaginable for both of us. She always felt a barrier in our relationship but did not fully understand it. The barrier was my sinful past, which God helped me to overcome. Now, when we are intimate, it is just between the two of us.

I spent many hours studying the Word of God, in prayer and fasting, seeking understanding. The Spirit of the Lord truly quickened me. I became stronger day by day in the knowledge of the truth. I learned to renew my mind with the word of God. I began to realign my thoughts and my conduct with the Word of God. I blindly believed God and committed to obey his instructions in the Bible. I began to take every thought captive to the obedience of Christ (2 Corinthians 10:3-5).

"For though we walk in the flesh, we do not war according to the flesh. For the weapons of our warfare are not carnal but mighty in God for pulling down strongholds, casting down arguments and every high thing that exalts itself against the knowledge of God, bringing every thought into captivity to the obedience of Christ."

I began to see myself in Jesus Christ and confessed God's word, *"I am crucified with Christ; nevertheless I live; yet not I, but Christ lives in me; and the life I live in the flesh, I live by the faith of the Son of God who loved me and gave Himself for me (Galatians 2:20). Therefore I can do all things through Christ Jesus who strengthens me. (Philippians 4:13).*

I learned about the righteousness of God, and I sought to understand what it means to be righteous and justified in the sight of God. This understanding of my justification through Christ Jesus changed my life and strengthened my walk with Him. I learned that I am reconciled with God and have peace with Him (Romans 5). I am now His son, He loves me and nothing can separate me from the love of God that is in Christ Jesus my Lord (Romans 8). When Satan brings condemning and sinful thoughts to my mind, I learn to resist them in the name of Jesus for James 4:7 states, *"Submit therefore to God; resist the devil and he will flee from you."* As I resist and cast out those negative thoughts in the name of Jesus using the Scriptures, the promise has always proven true: the devil flees from me! As I discovered my identity and authority in Christ, the word of God empowers me and set me free from the oppression of Satan.

My First Visit to Haiti After 16 Years

After the funeral of my mother in Haiti in 1988, I decided never to return to Haiti. The primary reason was that I felt powerless to make a difference in Haiti. I saw the suffering of the people, and I could not do very much to help them. There were very few success stories. My heart was broken to see many of my childhood friends in abject poverty. They had become parents without the resources to support their families. Living conditions were continuing to deteriorate. Indeed, it was painful to see young men and women so aged by the hardships of life that they were ready to die. I could look in the heart of the children and feel the sense of despair. When I spoke to young people, I could see their inner strength and determination to overcome their obstacles while trying to cope with their living conditions. I saw so clearly the agony of living a life without hope. They could not see the future. The meaning of life is hidden from them. They live one day at the time with their eyes seeking their next meal, while their bodies are hoping to find it, and their hearts longing to understand why they were created to live in such despair. Is this truly the meaning of life to simply live day by day like a wanderer without hope and without rest?

I finally returned to Haiti in August, 2004 after 16 years. One of my uncles came to visit me. I asked him about his oldest son who is in his forties. My uncle replied, "He is dropping them." I did not understand what he really meant. He then told me that his son has at least 10 children with different women, and he could not support them. This story is familiar across Haiti. Children are considered as family resources. They help with farming and other activities. When the parents become old, they expect their children to care for them since Haiti has no support system to care for the elderly.

During my return visit, I conducted three days of revival in my hometown. My ministry provided food to the people for the three days. My cousin Dina, a local doctor, provided free consultation and dispensed over-the-counter medicine I had brought with me. People walked many hours and miles from surrounding communities to come for the free consultation and medicine. I remember one specific case of a baby boy around one year old. He had a burning fever. The baby was trembling, and the mother said that he had been in that condition off and on for a few days. She did not have money to take him to the nearest clinic. No funds or the lack of funds is a normal way of life for many Haitians. Ironically, one of my brothers informed me after I returned to Belgium from the revival that some of the people in my community believed that I came to conduct a voodoo ceremony to honor the spirit "loa," who protected me during my deployments to two wars, "Operation Just cause in Panama" in 1989 and "Operation Desert Storm" in 1990. It saddened me that the people are in such spiritual darkness and their minds remained clouded with evil thoughts.

The Creation of My Ministry: Blessing and Healing Ministries, Inc.

The Beginning:

After my baptism in the Holy Spirit and the revelation of my vocation to preach the good news of Jesus Christ to the Haitian people, I began to take action to change my plans. I intended to stay in the army until the age of 62 and retire in Orlando, Florida. I figured by then I would be well-established financially.

After my conversion, my outlook on life changed completely, as I was firmly determined to please God for the rest of my life. Carolyn and I decided that we would need a non-profit organization as the channel for carrying out God's purpose for our family. Since we were praying for the blessings of God upon Haiti, and God had anointed me with the gift of healing, we decided to call the organization- <u>Blessing and Healing Ministries</u>. I wanted a slogan to identify the ministry. While visiting my brother Pierre in Miami, I woke up one morning with this slogan lingering in my mind "Jesus is the Answer." Thus, we confirmed the name of the organization as, <u>Blessing and Healing Ministries – Jesus is the Answer!</u>

Carolyn and I began to expand our family-style worship to her mother's house on Friday evenings. We drove several hours to Fayetteville, North Carolina from Fort Lee, Virginia and invited close friends and relatives to praise and worship God with us. I was filled with the joy of preaching God's word and praying for the sick. Truly, we are attempting to do great things for God's glory, and we are expecting great things from our faithful God who can neither lie nor fail!

Reaching Haiti for the Glory of God

Our Organization:

Blessing and Healing Ministries, Inc is a non-denominational Christian organization. This organization exists to glorify the Lord Jesus Christ. Learning and applying Biblical principles in our activities is an important expression of our identity.

Our Mission and Ministry To the Haitian People

Mission:

Lead the Haitian people to national repentance and faith in Jesus Christ.

Ministry:

We will preach the message of repentance and faith in Jesus Christ to Haitians in every community and geographical department throughout Haiti via radio, television, local community revival meetings, and outreach programs. We will minister to the critical needs of the nation by implementing social assistance programs to help achieve our mission.

We will build Christian Community Development Centers (CCDC). The CCDC complex will consist of an orphanage, Christian based schools: professional, technical and classical education, a medical clinic, a cafeteria, a recreation center, and a chapel. We will promote Christian based social activities, thereby young Haitians can be nurtured in a Christian environment in reverence of God. We will demonstrate our love to the Haitian people, and earn their trust. Through the teaching and preaching of the word of God, we will develop a new generation of Haitians who will revere God, despise corruption, and show compassion for one another.

May God Bless America!

After 25 years of active duty service in the United States Army, I retired on August 1, 2008 and returned to Haiti to preach the Good News of the kingdom of God and the name of Jesus to my people. I will always be grateful to the United States of America and pray for God's continued blessings upon this great nation. I have learned that the greatness of the United States is not in its strong military power or its advanced technological capabilities; rather, the United States is a great nation because anyone in America regardless of background, color, or race can hope, dream and, ultimately succeed. People can indeed dream in America, and more importantly they can fulfill these dreams with hard work, self-discipline, perseverance and faith in God. When I first joined the Army, I set four goals:

1. Complete 20 years in the Army and retire
2. Reach the highest rank in my field of service
3. Obtain a master degree
4. Save $1,000,000

On the day of my retirement, I looked back at these goals and gave praise and glory to God for helping me along the way. I have completed 25 years and 11 days, reached the rank of Chief Warrant Officer Four, the highest rank in my field in 1983 when I first set the objective. I have obtained two Masters degrees: Business Administration (MBA) and Logistics Management (MA); and also a Doctorate degree in Ministry (DMin). I did not achieve the $1,000,000 objective, but I found something much better — I found Jesus! Along the way, God has also blessed me with a beautiful and faithful woman of God to be my helper and my best friend – my wife Carolyn. I share this information as a mean to express my heartfelt gratitude to a gracious God who redeemed me from my sins.

America is not a perfect society; there are still social issues and challenges, but it is truly a nation of opportunities where a person is limited only by his or her ability to dream. I pray that God continues to protect and bless America!

Chapter 4

What Will It Take to Heal Haiti?

See, I set before you today life and prosperity, death and destruction. For I command you today to love the LORD your God, to walk in his ways, and to keep his commands, decrees and laws; then you will live and increase, and the LORD your God will bless you in the land you are entering to possess. But if your heart turns away and you are not obedient, and if you are drawn away to bow down to other gods and worship them, I declare to you this day that you will certainly be destroyed. You will not live long in the land you are crossing the Jordan to enter and possess. This day I call heaven and earth as witnesses against you that I have set before you life and death, blessings and curses. Now choose life, so that you and your children may live and that you may love the LORD your God, listen to his voice, and hold fast to him. For the LORD is your life, and he will give you many years in the land he swore to give to your fathers, Abraham, Isaac and Jacob.   (Deuteronomy 30:15-20)

The United Nations (UN) Is Not the Solution

The UN has been trying wholeheartedly to find the answer to Haiti's national crisis and other struggling nations without substantial success. The UN and various international organizations are busy dealing with crises such as disasters, wars, famine, and diseases around the world. In truth, the problems are numerous and complex, the cost is enormous, and the impact on human lives is catastrophic. In examining various crises around the world, I believe that the underlying problems are the same, but they are exhibited in different forms. The main problem is our separation from God because of our sins and continual violation of His principles for the welfare of humankind.

This book advocates a new approach in solving world crises. In countries where Christianity is accepted, implementation of the key recommendations of this book is guaranteed to bring positive results. If adequate resources are allocated to teach people to love God and their neighbors and encourage them to live by the principles that God our Creator provides in the Holy Bible, a better world will be the result: *"Righteousness exalts a nation, but sin is a disgrace to any people"* (Proverbs 14:34).

This world consists of nations and nations are made up of people created only by God. If we choose to deny the existence of God as the sole Creator of all things, our denial does not change the fact that He is the only true God and Creator of the universe. However, the *impact* of our ignorance and rejection of His existence is the problem that world governments are trying to contend and resolve.

The world is seeking a solution for Haiti and for many other countries that are confronting drastic socio-economic problems. The "lessons learned" in dealing with these socio-economic issues around the world have provided reasonable solutions. Yet, it appears that the conditions are not improving around the world. On the contrary, the problems seem to be progressively worse. This is not a pessimistic observation, but the reality of our world today. The lessons learned cannot be applied effectively to bring about positive changes from one nation to another in dealing with similar issues. The simple reason why the techniques and lessons learned are not transmissible is because the core issue has been ignored and the real solution underestimated and rejected. In Haiti, the central problem is demonic influences and continual transgressions against God's principles. The solution requires radical changes within the culture and belief system of the people. As mentioned earlier, all attempts to resolve Haiti's devastating living conditions have repeatedly failed. Despite millions of dollars donated to the Haitian Government and other nongovernmental organizations (NGO) for development and social assistance programs in Haiti, the arduous living conditions are not changed significantly. The collective efforts of the UN will likely continue to fail unless changes occur in the heart of the Haitian people, transformation that only God can perform.

In 1994, military forces of the UN debarked in Haiti for a peace mission and democratic reconstruction of the Haitian government. Ten years later, in 2004, the UN is once again engaged in a peacekeeping and democratic reform mission in Haiti. While I pray for the success of the ongoing UN mission in Haiti, I also know that Jesus Christ is the only permanent solution to Haiti's problems. Haitians, for many decades, have been relying on foreign aid, and in more recent years, set their hope on foreign intervention to help restore security, financial stability, and create better living conditions for the people. Nonetheless, after 200 years of independence, 47 national governments, 19 years of American occupation, two international military interventions, various overthrowing of appointed and elected governments, and millions of dollars in foreign aid to Haiti, there is no substantial evidence of improvement in the national living conditions. Haiti remains in a very poor state of existence. The poor are getting poorer, and the rich are getting richer; hopelessness and crime statistics are escalating. The world continues to try collectively to allocate resources to fix the external conditions, not realizing that the problems are internal rather than external. It is the hearts and minds of the people that need to be renewed before the people and subsequently the government can be impacted profoundly.

The world remains blind to the fact that the root cause of the socio-economic problems in Haiti is entirely spiritual. The battleground for the deliverance of Haiti is indeed the minds and hearts of the Haitian people. The corruption in government , the greed and selfishness in the private sector that discourage competition, the terror of kidnapping to obtain money, the burning of national landmarks and public buildings, and even the burning of human beings alive by angry mobs in Haiti are all the results of the wickedness that fills the hearts of many Haitians in a culture that encourages sinful practices and rebellion against God.

It is worth emphasizing that all reconstruction efforts in Haiti must include the task of transforming the hearts of the Haitian people by the renewing of their minds, their beliefs, and values through the teaching, preaching, and application of biblical principles. Any approach to improving the austere living conditions in Haiti, which does not include this vital task, will produce no lasting effect. It is essential that the minds of the people be reconditioned and their hearts be touched by the healing power of God's love. Such transformation requires the intervention of the Holy Spirit through influential Haitian political leaders to help guide the nation into righteousness and the fear of God.

A Haitian National Leader Equipped with Good Intentions Is Not the Solution

Haitian leaders are faced with overwhelming demonic influences in the administration of public functions. The reality is that a Haitian national leader, who is not in right standing with God and filled with the Holy Spirit, will not succeed against Satan's influences in this great spiritual battle to restore Haiti's national dignity and lead the nation to prosperity. In the Bible, the apostle Paul helps us to see clearly the magnitude of the problem of sin and the enormous need of the Holy Spirit's presence and leadership in our lives. In Romans 7:14-25, Paul explained how he was failing terribly under the bondage of sin:

> *We know that the Law is spiritual. But I am merely a human, and I have been sold as a slave to sin. In fact, I don't understand why I act the way I do. I don't do what I know is right. I do the things I hate. Although I don't do what I know is right, I agree that the Law is good. So I am not the one doing these evil things. The sin that lives in me is what does them. I know that my selfish desires won't let me do anything that is good. Even when I want to do right, I cannot. Instead of doing what I know is right, I do wrong. And so, if I don't do what I know is right, I am no longer the one doing these evil things. The sin that lives in me is what does them. The Law has shown me that something in me keeps me from doing what I know is right. With my whole heart I agree with the Law of God. But in every part of me I discover something fighting against my mind, and it makes me a prisoner of sin that controls everything I do. What a miserable person I am. Who will rescue me from this body that is doomed to die?* <u>*Thank God! Jesus*</u>

<u>Christ will rescue me.</u> *So with my mind I serve the Law of God, although my selfish desires make me serve the law of sin (emphasis added).*

We are all sinners in urgent need of Jesus to save us from the bondage of sin! No man in his own strength can resist Satan's power. This explains the cause of the failures of politicians who, in the beginning, had good intentions for the advancement of the country but fell into corruption and dishonorable conduct. We are strictly in a great fight of faith for the deliverance of Haiti from demonic influences that are keeping this nation in bondage of despair and poverty. Access to divine resources is a prerequisite for success in this warfare. It will take courage and boldness to make the changes necessary to foster a Christian Republic, eradicate corruption, and establish a strong and transparent system of accountability in all aspects of government.

It will take a Head of State full of faith and the power of the Holy Spirit to dethrone Satan and remove his strongholds from Haiti. This leader must exemplify godly living, trustworthiness, and unambiguous commitment to honor God while serving the Haitian people. An undisciplined, unfaithful individual in his or her personal life will very likely become undisciplined and unfaithful in managing public affairs. If one is not faithful in managing a small task, he or she cannot be trusted with greater responsibility. Jesus said in Luke 16:10: *"whoever can be trusted with very little can also be trusted with much, and whoever is dishonest with very little will be dishonest with much."* The Haitian people should apply this principle in selecting their political leaders. There are many competent and educated Haitians around the world who want to return to Haiti to invest and serve the nation. They are waiting and hoping for changes in Haiti.

Haiti Can Be Healed!

God says in the Bible: "I am looking for a man among them who would repair the wall and stand in the gap before me on behalf of the nation, so I would not destroy it, but I found no one (Ezekiel 22:30)." God heard the prayers of intercession for Haiti. He has determined His own time to liberate the Haitian people from hopelessness, only because of His unchanging love and faithfulness to those who trust in Him. After all, Jesus' precious blood was shed for the Haitian people as well. However, they need to come to the knowledge of the truth on one accord. Like the citizens of Nineveh in the book of Jonah in the Bible, the Haitian people must repent and turn to God, while performing deeds appropriate to repentance. When the prophet Jonah told the people of the city of Nineveh of God's judgment against them, the people believed God. The Bible says that the Ninevites declared a fast, and all of them, from the greatest to the least, put on sackcloth. When the news reached the King of Nineveh, he rose from his throne, took off his royal robes, covered himself with sackcloth and sat down in the dust. When God saw their actions and how they turned from their evil ways, He had compassion on them and therefore did not carry out His threat against their nation (Jonah 3:4-10).

Spiritual Solution

Haiti has reached a phase of final decision. The Haitian people must examine themselves and reflect on the current national conditions and the future of our nation. The Haitian people must decide either to turn to Jesus Christ to be delivered from the penalty of sins or to continue on the current path. The first option undoubtedly will bring positive outcomes and hope. On the other hand, failure to reconcile the nation with God through repentance will surely bring more destruction and misery on the nation. The decision to resolve the spiritual problems identified in this book should be the first step towards a lasting solution to Haiti's national problems. After all, Haiti has tried unsuccessfully almost all possible solutions to resolve the socio-economic issues that have paralyzed the nation and disgraced the Haitian people.

God Needs a "Nehemiah" for the Reconstruction of Haiti!

The preaching of the gospel of Jesus Christ by itself is not sufficient to bring about the transformation and the healing of Haiti. The gospel is God's power to save and change a person's heart. However, God also needs a loyal servant, a man or woman of prayer, in a position of national authority to influence policies, make changes in the functioning of the government, and faithfully manage the country's resources for God's Glory and the welfare of the Haitian people. This truth is the missing link and the greatest obstacles to the Gospel in Haiti. God needs more faithful Christians in position of influence in Haiti. Many faithful Christians refuse to get engaged in the political process because of corruption and the negative associations with the political system. Sadly, some of the Christians who chose to serve in the government quickly abandoned God and His principles. President Aristide used his influence as Head of State to legalize voodoo. Likewise, having been a Catholic priest, if he had God's interest in his heart, he could have used his influence to lead the nation to national repentance and faith in Jesus Christ. Haiti has all the resources necessary to ensure the welfare of its people. Unfortunately, without a "Nehemiah," a person of national influence to rebuild the nation and glorify the name of Jesus Christ, the Gospel will continue to produce marginal effects in the Haitian society.

Most Haitians today recognize that the nation is heading in the wrong direction and needs to be rescued from the current condition of hopelessness. They are seeking solutions and assistance but from the wrong sources. Haiti has an urgent need to be led to the only source of life from whom the Haitian people can obtain genuine peace for their soul and the healing of their land: <u>the Lord Jesus Christ</u>!

Spiritual problems can only be solved by using spiritual principles that God has established. Sin contains built-in judgment and its punishment will surely find and overtake violators of God's principles. The most regrettable aspect of sin is our separation from God. Apart from God we are deprived of life. He created us and established Himself as our source of joy and fulfillment. The apostle Paul made it clear in Acts 17:28 that God is the environment of our lives – for in Him we live, we walk, and exist. That explains why life is so unfulfilling for so many people. Some people have wealth and fame and everything to live for, yet they are miserable because they are living in an environment apart from God – their source of life! The prerequisite for victory in Haiti over poverty and despair is the restoration of a national relationship with God. Only God's prescription for sin will work. Jesus says in Luke 13:3, "Unless you repent you shall likewise perish." His promise to sinners is if they confess and repent of their sin, He will forgive them. Accordingly, the Haitian people must repent of their iniquities and seek God's forgiveness and mercy. The nation must be led to national repentance, and God will send trustworthy leaders to serve and lead the people in justice.

It Will Take Divine Intervention Through the Work of Faithful Christians!

The current desperate conditions in Haiti are undoubtedly the result of transgressions against established divine principles. Therefore, the solution requires divine intervention to restore the hearts of the Haitian people, and heal the nation. However, God needs Christians full of faith and the power of the Holy Spirit to represent Him to the Haitian people, in politics, business, school system, news media, music industry, and other areas. Through faithful Christians, God wants to demonstrate His compassion for the afflicted, His love for the poor and His power that the Most High is sovereign over the kingdoms of men and gives it to whomever He chooses (Daniel 4:25). After all, Christians are commanded to make disciples of nations and to teach them to observe all that Christ commanded (Matthew 28:19). It is a Christian responsibility to contribute in ensuring that godly people are in position of authority and to pray for their success.

I spent the summer of 2008 in Haiti and witnessed one of the worst natural disaster the nation has ever suffered. I spent my first forty days in my hometown of Chambellan in fasting and prayer to seek God's instruction for my assignment. I visited most of the local churches. It saddened my heart to see the ineffectiveness of the gospel in that community as it is throughout Haiti. The Haitian people hear the gospel. There are many radio stations, international organizations, missionary activities that are transmitting the gospel in Haiti. Yet, the people are increasingly less compassionate and more cynical and divided because of the influence of the political system and lack of economic opportunities. I saw no applauding changes in the lives of the people and no significant success stories for me to acknowledge. I witnessed increased despair, many more children in poverty and a young population very doubtful of the future.

Today, many churches throughout Haiti are filled with people but are void of God's power. I believe the ineffectiveness of the Word of God in Haiti is partially the result of many lukewarm Christians who are preaching the Gospel. Their hearts are not fully committed to the work of the Lord. Therefore, the Holy Spirit is hindered in His work of convicting Haitians of sins and empowering them to resist Satan's temptations. It is the Spirit of God who touches people's hearts to bring about renewal and transformation. Haitians are looking for role models and trustworthy people to lead them in righteousness. Christians are ambassadors of Jesus Christ. We must display absolute integrity and convey the truth of the love of God through our deeds in the midst of the people. The need for spiritual revival is urgent and essential in the healing process of the nation. This promise remains true today and will prove profitable: *"If my people, who are called by my name, will humble themselves and pray and seek my face and turn from their wicked ways, then will I hear from heaven and will forgive their sin and will heal their land"* (2 Chronicles 7:14). God wants to revive His people first, in order for them to become a source of light and blessing in their communities for His glory.

The Message to the Haitian People: "Repent, Be Baptized, and Filled with the Holy Spirit!"

Haitians, in every community across the nation, must hear this message and be invited to receive Jesus into their hearts. This call to national repentance and faith in Jesus Christ is the truth that will liberate the Haitian people and transform their miserable circumstances.

Before my ultimate conversion to Christianity, I learned from my past commitment to Satan and voodoo beliefs that Haitians have great faith. It takes great faith to trust Satan especially after years of misery and to remain committed to a master that causes only sorrow. This same level of faith in the finished work of Christ on the cross can produce amazingly positive results in our lives.

For all of their lives, Haitians have seen the wickedness of Satan for he is the father of lies who came to kill, steal, and destroy. The people have been told stories of individuals killed through the practice of voodoo. Many people have personally experienced the loss of loved ones through witchcraft and other evil practices. They believe deeply in the power of Satan to kill them. They have also heard of the power of God to heal the sick and raise the dead, and the abundant life that Jesus promises, but very few people have experienced such manifestation of God's power. God can be trusted to keep His promises and perform His word. The Bible clearly affirms that God is faithful. 1 John 1:9 states, "If you confess your sins, God is faithful and just to forgive you and cleanse you of all unrighteousness." This is an eternal promise to all people. Haiti can be forgiven and cleansed if the Haitian people would heed the call to national repentance. The blood of Jesus on the cross is indeed powerful and available to cleanse the people's hearts and to bring a time of refreshment upon the land. The Gospel of Jesus Christ is the power of God to save those who hear it, believe it and, practice it. I pray that the Haitian people seize this period of change and renewal that God has decreed for the nation to repent and turn to our Lord and Savior Jesus Christ for the healing of our land.

Chapter 5

The Road Map to Haiti's Deliverance

The hand of the Lord was upon me, and he brought me out by the Spirit of the Lord and set me in the middle of a valley; it was full of bones. He led me back and forth among them, and I saw a great many bones on the floor of the valley, bones that were very dry. He asked me, "Son of man, can these bones live?" I said, "O Sovereign Lord, you alone know." Then he said to me, "Prophesy to these bones and say to them, 'Dry bones, hear the word of the Lord! This is what the Sovereign Lord says to these bones: I will make breath enter you, and you will come to life. I will attach tendons to you and make flesh come upon you and cover you with skin; I will put breath in you, and you will come to life. Then you will know that I am the Lord.'" (Ezekiel 37: 1-6)

Biblical Perspective

Haiti's widely practice of voodoo, idolatry, fornication, and adultery is absolutely contrary to God's principles and provision for happy, prosperous, and righteous living according to the Bible. These practices are the core features in the Haitian culture, and they have been prevalent throughout Haiti's history. It is evident that the Bible provides recurring situations of God's blessing upon nations and individuals that obey His principles. In contrast, the wrath of God rests heavily on nations and individuals that show disregard to His ordinances. As mentioned earlier, God's principles contain inherent judgment: blessings for obeying them and curses for violating them.

God created man in His image and gave man dominion over all His creation and blessed them (Genesis 1: 26-31). The disobedience of man introduced sin in the world. God gave humanity four basic institutions: the family, human government, Israel, and the church. Each of these institutions demonstrates an attribute of God. The family demonstrates the unity of God (Genesis 2:24). Through the family, God sought to bring into proper relationship the world with Himself. Human government illustrates the judgment of God (Romans 13:1-2). God's purpose in human government is that it serves as both a custodian and an enforcer of His eternal law. Israel illustrates the election of God (Romans 9:1-18). Israel was to be a channel of God's blessing as well as a recipient. The church illustrates the love of God (Ephesians 5:22-27).(4) For God so loved the world, He gave His only begotten Son, that whosoever believes in Him should not perish but have everlasting life. (John 3:16).

The Biblical history of the nation of Israel represents a marvelous outlook of God's graciousness working through promises, miracles, blessings, and judgments. Israel began as only a promise to Abraham (Genesis 12:2). For over four hundred years, the people of Israel relied on that promise, especially during the period of bondage in Egypt. Finally, in God's perfect timing, He brought the nation out of Egypt with the greatest series of miracles in the Bible. Since these events constituted the miraculous birth of the nation of Israel, it is to this great act of redemption that the nation always looks back as the foremost example of God's care for His people (Hosea 11:1, Psalms 77:14-20). Once God had redeemed Israel, He established His covenant with them. The covenant foretells gracious blessings for obedience and severe judgment for disobedience (Deuteronomy 28). Israel's history can be divided according to the nation's obedience or disobedience. The history of Israel clearly shows that the nation was indeed blessed when the people obeyed God and penalized when they disobeyed His statutes. The practical review of Israel's history sets forth examples to be followed or avoided and also serves a model for all ages of God's kindness and mercy toward His people (Psalms 103:14). The Bible in 1 Corinthians 10: 6-9 clearly illustrates how the nation of Israel and its people forfeited their liberty as a result of their disobedience to God's ordinances. They lusted after evil things, as they become idolaters while committing sexual immoralities. These historically sinful practices such as idolatry and sexual immoralities that caused many nations to perish are widely accepted and embedded in the Haitian culture today. The Bible condemns idolatry and the practice of witchcraft as abominations to God and prescribes the ultimate punishment of death (Deuteronomy 18, Leviticus 20). According to Psalms 96:5, there is only one God, and any other god is a demon. (5)

The Book of Nehemiah - A Model for the Haitian People

In the Holy Bible, the book of Nehemiah clearly correlates with the current situation in Haiti and presents a strong alternative solution to Haiti's national problems. Nehemiah provides an exceptional example of the efforts, discipline, and leadership that are required to rebuild the infrastructures in Haiti, renew the minds of the Haitian people with the Word of God, and assist them in the revival of their traditions.

The book of Nehemiah describes cold-hearted defiance toward God by the people of Israel during the four hundred years before Christ, during which there was no revelation from God. Consequently, similar to Haiti today, the Jewish people and their land suffered enormously. The people had a mind to work, but they needed a selfless and faithful leader to guide and care for them. It was not until the people repented and committed themselves to God that their minds were rehabilitated, and their land also became fruitful.

The book of Nehemiah demonstrates God's compassion and mercy as He answered Nehemiah's prayers and supplications on behalf of the people of Israel. Acknowledging the sins and disobedience of the people of Israel against God's ordinances, Nehemiah fervently prayed to God for the forgiveness of sins and the restoration of Jerusalem. Nehemiah's concern for the welfare of Jerusalem and its inhabitants prompted him to take bold action. He prayed and then secured King Artaxerxes' permission, provision, and protection for the massive project of rebuilding the walls. Nehemiah returned to his homeland and challenged his countrymen to rise up and rebuild the shattered wall of Jerusalem. The wall of Jerusalem represented the fortification, protection, and security of the city. In spite of opposition and threats, God's faithfulness and power enabled Nehemiah to successfully complete the task of rebuilding the wall of Jerusalem in a relatively short period of time. However, the task of reviving and reforming the people's culture and beliefs by contrast within the rebuilt wall demanded years of Nehemiah's godly life and leadership.

Nehemiah demonstrated courage, compassion for the oppressed, integrity, godliness, and selflessness. He gave up the luxury and ease of the palace as the cup-bearer of the Persian King to help His people. He was a dedicated layman who had the right priorities and concern for God's work. He was able to encourage and rebuke at the right times.

Nehemiah was strong in prayer and gave all glory and credit to God. Nehemiah identified with the plight of his people. He came with the specific mission and fulfilled it, and his life was characterized by prayerful dependence on God.

The work began immediately on the wall and its gates, with people building portions corresponding to where they were living. However, opposition quickly arose, first in the form of mockery and then in the form of conspiracy when the works were progressing at an alarming rate. Nehemiah overcame threats of force by setting half of the people on military watch and half on construction. While external opposition continued to mount, internal opposition also surfaced. The wealthier Jews abused and oppressed the people and sold them into slavery. Nehemiah again dealt with the problems by means of prayers and action. He also led by example when he sacrificed his governor's salary. In spite of deceits, slander, and treachery, Nehemiah continued to trust in God and to press on with singleness of mind until the work was completed. The task was accomplished in an incredible fifty-two days, and even his enemies recognized it could only have been accomplished with the help of God.

This biblical story reflects Nehemiah's success in his mission to reconstruct the wall of Jerusalem, renew the covenant with God, and reform the people's culture and beliefs. As governor, Nehemiah also established firm civil authority while working with other trusted spiritual leaders to build the people spiritually and morally so that the restoration would be complete. He fostered physical and political reconstruction and led the people into moral reforms. The reconstruction of the wall was followed by consecration and consolidation of the people. Ezra was the trusted leader of the spiritual revival.

After the completion of the wall, Ezra stood on special wooden podium to read God's ordinances to the people. The people responded with weeping, confession, obedience, and rejoicing. The Levites and priests led them in a great prayer that surveyed God's past work of deliverance and loyalty on behalf of His people and magnified God's attributes of holiness, justice, mercy, and love. The covenant was then renewed with God as the people committed themselves to obey God's commandments. The Book of Nehemiah Chapter nine reflects the following confession by the people of Israel for their sins and the iniquities of their fathers:

On the twenty-fourth day of the same month, the Israelites gathered together, fasting and wearing sackcloth and having dust on their heads. Those of Israelite descent had separated themselves from all foreigners. They stood in their places and confessed their sins and the wickedness of their fathers. They stood where they were and read from the Book of the Law of the LORD their God for a quarter of the day, and spent another quarter in confession and in worshipping the LORD their God. Standing on the stairs were the Levites: Jeshua, Bani, Kadmiel, Shebaniah, Bunni, Sherebiah, Bani and Kenani, who called with loud voices to the LORD their God. And the Levites: Jeshua, Kadmiel, Bani, Hashabneiah, Sherebiah, Hodiah, Shebaniah and Pethahiah said: Stand up and praise the LORD your God, who is from everlasting to everlasting. Blessed be your glorious name, and may it be exalted above all blessing and praise. You alone are the LORD. You made the heavens, even the highest heavens, and all their starry host, the earth and all that is on it, the seas and all that is in them. You give life to everything, and the multitudes of heaven worship you. You are the LORD God, who chose Abram and brought him out of Ur of the Chaldeans and named him Abraham. You found his heart faithful to you, and you made a covenant with him to give to his descendants the land of the Canaanites, Hittites, Amorites, Perizzites, Jebusites and Girgashites. You have kept your promise because you are righteous. You saw the suffering of our forefathers in Egypt; you heard their cry at the Red Sea. You sent miraculous signs and wonders against Pharaoh, against all his officials and all the people of his land, for you knew how arrogantly the Egyptians treated them. You made a name for yourself, which remains to this day. You divided the sea before them, so that they passed through it on dry ground, but you hurled their pursuers into the depths, like a stone into mighty waters. By day you led them with a pillar of cloud, and by night with a pillar of fire to give them light on the way they were to take. You came down on Mount Sinai; you spoke to them from heaven. You gave them regulations and laws that are just and right, and decrees and commands that are good. You made known to them your holy Sabbath and gave them commands, decrees and laws through your servant Moses. In their hunger you gave them bread from heaven and in their thirst you brought them water from the rock; you told them to go in and take possession of the land you had sworn with uplifted hand to give them. But they, our forefathers, became arrogant and stiff-necked, and did not obey your commands. They refused to listen and failed to remember the miracles you performed among them. They became stiff-necked and in their rebellion appointed a leader in order to return to their slavery. But you are a forgiving God, gracious and compassionate, slow to anger and abounding in love. Therefore you did not desert them, even when they cast for themselves an image of a calf and said, 'This is your god, who brought you up out of Egypt,' or when they committed awful blasphemies. Because of your great compassion you did not *abandon them in the desert. By day the pillar of cloud did not cease to guide them on their path, nor the pillar of fire by night to shine on the way they were to take. You gave your good Spirit to instruct them. You did not withhold your manna from their mouths, and you gave them water for their thirst. For forty years you sustained them in the desert; they lacked nothing, their clothes did not wear out nor did their feet become swollen. You gave them kingdoms and nations, allotting to them even the remotest frontiers. They took over the country of Sihon king of Heshbon and the country of Og king of Bashan. You made their sons as numerous as the stars in the sky, and you brought them into the land that you told their fathers to enter and possess. Their sons went in and took possession of the land. You subdued before them the Canaanites, who lived in the land; you handed the Canaanites over to them, along with their kings and the peoples of the land, to deal with them as they pleased. They captured fortified cities and fertile land; they took possession of houses filled with all kinds of good things, wells already dug, vineyards, olive groves and fruit trees in abundance. They ate to the full and were well-nourished; they revelled in your great goodness. But they were disobedient and rebelled against you; they put your law behind their backs. They killed your prophets, who had admonished them in order to turn them back to you; they committed awful blasphemies. So you handed them over to their enemies, who oppressed them. But when they were oppressed they cried out to you. From heaven you heard them, and in your great compassion you gave them deliverers, who rescued them from the hand of their enemies. But as soon as they were at rest, they again did what was evil in your sight. Then you abandoned them to the hand of their enemies so that they ruled over them. And when they cried out to you again, you heard from heaven, and in your compassion you delivered them time after time. You warned them to return to your law, but they became arrogant and disobeyed your commands. They sinned against your ordinances, by which a man will live if he obeys them. Stubbornly they turned their backs on you, became stiff-necked and refused to listen. For many years you were patient with them. By your Spirit you admonished them through your prophets. Yet they paid no attention, so you handed them over to the neighboring peoples. But in your great mercy you did not put an end to them or abandon them, for you are a gracious and merciful God. Now therefore, O our God, the great, mighty and awesome God, who keeps his covenant of love, do not let all this hardship seem trifling in your eyes— the hardship that has come upon us, upon our kings and leaders, upon our priests and prophets, upon our fathers and all your people, from the days of the kings of Assyria until today. In all that has happened to us, you have been just; you have acted faithfully, while we did wrong. Our kings, our leaders, our priests and our fathers did not follow your law; they did not pay attention to your commands or the warnings you gave them. Even while they were in their kingdom, enjoying your great goodness to them in the spacious and fertile land you gave them, they did not serve you or turn from their evil ways. But see, we are slaves today, slaves in the land you gave our forefathers so that they could eat its fruit and the other good things it produces. Because of our sins, its abundant harvest goes to the kings you have placed over us. They rule over our bodies and our cattle as they please. We are in great distress. In view of all this, we are making a binding agreement, putting it in writing, and our leaders, our Levites and our priests are affixing their seals to it.*

According to the Holy Bible, there is no authority except that which God has established (Romans 13:1). As reflected throughout the Bible, when the nation of Israel displayed obedience to God's ordinances, the people enjoyed prosperity. Furthermore, God anointed and sent strong and faithful leaders to lead the nation. In contrast, during the times of disobedience, the nation suffered defeat and desolation, and God allowed the people to be led by uncaring and selfish leaders. Disobedience to God's ordinances for the proper functioning of humanity engenders trouble to any nation. When a nation forfeits God's grace and favors because of sinful traditions and practices, the ultimate price is destruction resulting from poor government administration and corruption leading to poverty and other social ills. For example, voodoo, idolatry, fornication, and adultery are widely accepted traditions and practices in some countries in West Africa. Consequently, poverty and poor government administration are widespread in those nations. Haiti inherited its voodoo practices from Benin, where a great majority of Haitian descendants came from as a result of the slave trade. Similarly to Haiti, Benin continues today its wide practice of voodoo worship. Likewise, both nations have high poverty rates. In contrast, the United States of America was founded on strong Christian principles. As a result, God blessed America tremendously. The statement, "In God We Trust," provides a clear symbol and a great testimony of the nation's founders' deep reverence for God.

Chapter 6

The Reconstruction of Haiti

Unless the Lord builds the house, they labor in vain who build it; unless the Lord guards the city, the watchman keeps awake in vain.
(Psalms 127:1)

May God Bless Haiti!

The reconstruction process must start with national repentance and faith in Jesus Christ as Lord and Savior of Haiti. Jesus must be the foundation of this new Republic. King Solomon well expressed this sentiment this way: "Unless *the Lord builds the house, they labor in vain who build it; unless the Lord guards the city, the watchman keeps awake in vain*" (Psalms 127:1). King David wrote in Psalms 33:12, "*How blessed is the nation whose God is the LORD, the people whom he has chosen to be his special possession.*"

Political and Socio-economic Solution

As the first black independent country of the world, Haiti lost its opportunity to have an impact on the world scene for the glory of God. As a model nation against oppression, Haiti can once again become a nation of testimony of God's unchanging love and faithfulness.

This book reveals another great opportunity for the Haitian people to glorify God by establishing Haiti as a Christian Republic, a nation founded on biblical principles. Certainly, Haiti can become the first nation to officially honor the Lord Jesus Christ and publicly proclaim Him as the Savior of our people. The Haitian people can accomplish this objective by following the example of the Ninivites as quoted earlier (Jonah 3:1-10). It will take national efforts by the Haitian people working together to rebuild their communities.

God has the last word. Thus, Satan will be defeated, and Haitians will truly be a free people under the care and in the favor of God. God has the power to transform Haiti's problems for the good of the nation, not only for Haiti but also for other nations who are also buried in poverty because of their rejection of God's eternal principles.

National Political Process

God will surely send someone for this period of renewal and change in Haiti, to serve and lead the nation in love, compassion, and righteousness to the glory of the Lord Jesus Christ. God will confirm this servant and his or her ministry with undeniable miracles. Once this individual whom God has ordained for this time in Haiti's History is revealed and confirmed, he or she should be elected as President of Haiti for five years with opportunity for reelection. This leader should be entrusted and given unobstructed authority to make drastic changes during his or her first term in office. This person should be allowed to appoint his or her ministers and advisors, State Governors, City Mayors without hindrance and opposition. These key leaders will assist the President in laying a strong foundation upon which the "New Haiti" will be built. At the end of the five-year term, the nation and the people will be well-prepared for national elections to elect their Mayors, Deputies, and others. There is a great need for national efforts to teach the people their civic responsibilities as citizens and the value of electing an individual to represent them.

Five Years Reconstruction Objectives

1) Government Reforms: Reconcile the nation with God through national repentance.

- Implement decrees to reflect Biblical principles and Christian values as the basis of national living standards.
- Implement community programs to effectively address moral and cultural values and issues that have negatively affected the national life.
- Restore government accountability and transparency in the administration of public affairs.
- Implement strong ethical standards and training of government employees to eliminate corruption and inefficiency in the administration of public affairs.
- Implement programs to strengthen democratic principles, and emphasize the love of country, and citizenship responsibilities.
- Teach and prepare the people to properly exercise their right to vote.
- Establish safeguards to prevent intimidation and bribery by candidates and political parties.
- Restore national honor and the people's trust in the Haitian Government.

2) Management of Government Affairs at National Level:

The Executive Branch: The President of Haiti is the Head of State and Commander in Chief of the

Armed Forces of the Republic. The President will appoint a Vice-President, the members of his or her ministerial cabinet, and the regional governors. The Vice-President is responsible for the operation of the government and assumes the Presidency under any unforeseen emergency when the President is unable to fulfill his functions. The President is responsible for enforcing the laws and representing the Haitian people at international functions. The government will establish Haitian embassies to assure diplomatic relations and national interest overseas.

The government will create a National Board of Executive Elders or Visionaries consisting of the brightest individuals in the nation with expertise in every discipline (e.g. Education, health, security, finances, etc.). This national board of visionaries will consist of the Chief Elder from each ministerial department. They will serve as staff and advisors to the Vice-president of the republic.

Each ministerial department will create a Board of Elders consisting of ten expert individuals with experience relating to the functions of the department. As stated, the Chief Elder from each ministerial department will serve on the National Board of Executive Elders. These ministerial boards of Elders will organize, coordinate, implement and administer measures and focus groups to study problems affecting national interests and provide recommendation to the respective cabinet minister of the department for action. Each expert Elder from a ministerial department will be assigned as liaison for one of the ten States or regions in the Republic to help coordinate regional issues at national level. This Elder will work closely with the State Governor and State's Board of Elders and other officials. The national budget will include detailed projects and programs for each geographical department to facilitate transparency and ensure the well-being of cities and provinces throughout the nation

The Legislative Branch: The legislature will be composed of Deputies representing each county of the Republic. The number of Deputies will be based on the numbers of counties in a region. Members will form one National Assembly of Deputies or House of Representatives. A member of the National Assembly of Deputies will be elected for four years. The Head of a regional delegation will be chosen by the members of that region. The allocation of administrative posts in the National Assembly of Deputies is determined by internal selection process. The role of a Deputy will be dedicated to implement the laws of the nation and ensure the interests of the city and the region represented. In general, the National Assembly of Deputies has no authority to disapprove the President's choice for any post, merely for political motive, without valid reasons pertaining to records, qualifications, and character of the person chosen by the President.

The Judicial Branch: The Minister of Justice is responsible for establishing the courts, police stations, and in general the administration of justice in the nation. He or she will appoint judges with the President's approval. The Supreme Court of the nation will consist of seven judges appointed for a term of ten years. Lower court judges are appointed for a term of five years. All judges are appointed on the basis of qualification and good report. When evidence of misconduct is provided, the National Assembly of Deputies can remove a Supreme Court Judge with the concurrence of 90% of the members. The Minister of Justice can remove a lower court judge with the concurrence of 5 out of 7 of the Supreme Court Judges.

3) Management of Government Affairs at Regional Level: The regional governor is the Chief Executive and the representative of the President of the Republic in the region. The Governor is responsible for the administration of all regional affairs. Each regional Governor will appoint an Inspector General and create a Regional Board of Elders consisting of expert individuals. The number of Elders at the regional level will be based on the number of counties in the region. Each Regional Elder will serve as liaison for the Municipal Visionaries Team in each city within a county. The Senior Regional Elder will serve as liaison to coordinate regional issues with the corresponding Board of Ministerial Elders.

4) Management of Government Affairs at City Level: The City Mayor is responsible for the administration of municipal affairs. The Regional Governor in collaboration with the City Mayor will also create a Municipal Board of Elders. The number of Elders at city level will be based on the number of sections in the city, but not less than three Elders. This team will be composed of wise individuals in various fields. They will identify problems, resources, and opportunities in the municipality and assist the Mayor and other city leaders with the administration and development of the city.

5) Requirements and Selection of Elders at All Levels: An Elder must possess extensive formal training and experience in the related field, the best minds in the nation! Also competent young Haitians, zealous and of good report can serve as elders. This position will not be affected by political changes. Service as Elders at all levels of government is for a term of three years with automatic renewal opportunities.

6) Government Accountability and Reporting Requirements: The government will create the position of Chief Inspector General (CIG) to be appointed by the President. The CIG will be provided a team of Elders and experts in every discipline to conduct inspections of all areas of public administration. The CIG's inspections will identify shortcomings and misdeeds (fraud, waste and abuse) for immediate resolution and also recognize outstanding public servants for national recognition. The CIG reports directly to the Vice-President of the Republic and will be adequately funded and empowered to carry out his or her functions without political hindrance.

- The CIG will provide quarterly reports to the Vice-President.
- The Team of Elders will provide quarterly reports to appropriate authority.
- The Vice-President of the Republic, assisted by each Cabinet Minister, will provide quarterly updates to the nation via national radio, television, and official newspapers.
- The President of the Republic will officially address the nation annually on the 2nd of January to present his programs and vision for the nation.
- Each Regional Vice-Governor, assisted by the Regional Inspector General, will provide quarterly reports to the region via national radio and newspaper.
- The Regional Governor will address the region annually via the national radio, television and newspaper on the 18th of May to present his vision for the region.
- City Mayors will coordinate town meetings at least semi-annually in December and July, or as needed to respond to local issues. The result of the town meeting will be recorded and forwarded through the Region Board of Elders to the Governor.
- Reports at all levels of government will include current issues, ongoing projects, status of projects, status of funds and other resources.

7) Public Education: The government must reform the education system to ensure the following:

- The right to a free education at all levels is guaranteed to everyone living in the territory of the Republic.
- All children across the nation have access to education beginning at the age of four years. Students may be given opportunities to attend classes in the evening as a means to obtain access to education while the government builds new schools.
- Both public and private schools must achieve national standards within five years.
- In primary school all classrooms must be adequately equipped and should not exceed forty students. The government must cooperate with private schools to ensure their success.
- Decentralize educational opportunities in Port-au-Prince. Establish technical and university level education in all ten regions of the Republic to minimize the economic impact on parents that are forced to send their children to Port-au-Prince because of lack of educational opportunities in their region.
- Build public libraries in every city with computers and internet access to facilitate research and encourage reading.
- Regional Governors are responsible for ensuring that their regions meet national standards for education.
- Implement mandatory Bible study program at all levels of education.
- All Haitian students must be able to speak fluent French by the end of primary school.
- Expand capacities of public universities to enroll and graduate more students primarily in the field of medicine and agronomy.
- Implement measures to ensure public universities offer doctorate degree programs.
- Implement measures to provide scholarships for

Haitian students to study medicine, engineering, and various technological and scientific fields abroad. Enforce strict accountability measures through Haitian embassies to oversee these students' activities, and ensure upon returning to Haiti, they are given opportunities to apply their skills.

- Increase teachers' pay as incentives to attract quality teachers.

8) National Security and the Fight Against Corruption:
Establish the Armed Forces of the Republic of Haiti with strong measures to prevent coup d'état. The minister of national security is responsible for oversight of military activities.

- The armed forces of the Republic will comprise three branches of service: The Army, the National Military Police, and the Special Forces. The Army will consist of combat forces such as Infantry and Artillery.
- The National Military Police will have a dual military and civilian mission.
- The Special Forces will be composed of soldiers with diverse talents. These soldiers are capable of providing logistical support, air defense, responding to natural disasters, monitoring the maritime boundaries of the territory of the republic, and organizing intelligence operations and investigation of crimes.
- The government must provide adequate compensation and establish strong and strict measures to prevent corruption and crime within the organization. Implement aggressive and severe penalties against all forms of crime.

9) Mandatory Public Service:
Public service is compulsory for all Haitians when they turn 18 years old and have completed high school or graduated from a public university. All young Haitians will be required to perform two years of public service to the nation in the military. Regional Governors may develop and imple-

ment substituted public service programs to satisfy this requirement.

10) Agriculture: Create incentives to encourage farmers to return to agriculture. Develop a plan to modernize agricultural tools and equipment to facilitate farming, minimize manual efforts of farmers, and also increase agricultural production. Create incentives for graduating students in the field of agriculture to return to rural areas to work with local farmers. Implement a system of "Micro agri-loan" to help farmers obtain money to buy seeds and prepare their harvest season.

11) Keep Haiti Beautiful and Protect Our Environment: Create a partnership with non-profit organizations focusing on reforestation.
- Take measures to protect and purify water sources and ensure that our citizens have access to drinking water in a convenient manner.
- Take urgent measures to explore, develop, and implement alternatives to the use of wood as a primary source of energy for cooking and heating.
- Establish standards and permit procedures for the construction of houses. Establish requirements for proper disposal of trash.

12) Infrastructure:

Electricity: Develop partnership with private investors to facilitate access to electricity without interruption in every city.

Major roads and ports: Prioritize the renovation and construction of paved roads, bridges, regional seaports, and airports throughout the country to facilitate trade.

13) Medical: Access to health care is a guaranteed right for all Haitian citizens. Regional Governors are responsible for ensuring their regions meet national health standards. Each city must have a Community Health Care Center (CHCC) that can effectively treats the most common cases of diseases such as tuberculosis, malaria, typhoid, and perform minor surgeries. These CHCC must be equipped with adequate laboratories and pharmacy support. Region Governors and City Mayors will ensure health clinics are established in remote areas to respond to emergencies such as injury, premature births, etc. Invest in preventive measures and ensure vaccination of all Haitians for various diseases. CHCC directors will establish a system of community health education programs to emphasize good health practices and prevent the transmission of contagious and sexually transmitted diseases.

14) News and Information: All news media and journalists will be registered with the government. The government will guarantee free speech, encourage journalism, and take strong action to protect journalists from any type of aggression. Journalists are the eyes and the voice of the people.

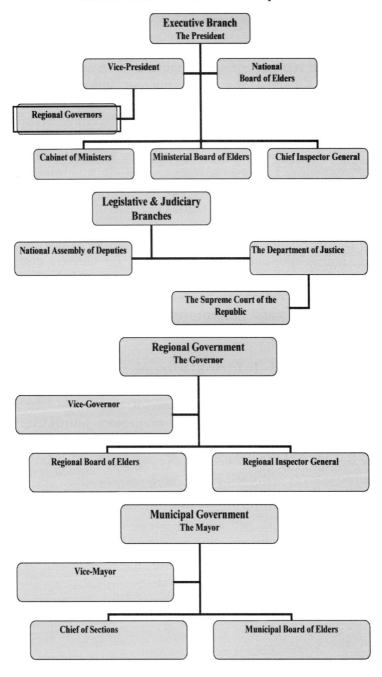

Armed Forces of the Republic of Haiti

Army
- Ground Combat Forces
- Military Academy
- Military Training Facilities

National Military Police
- Military Functions
- Civilian Law enforcement Functions

Special Operations Forces
- Maritime Operations & Surveillance of National Territory
- Intelligence
- Criminal Investigations
- Logistics Support
- Air Support
  - Disaster Response Team

Allocation of Military Ressources			
States / Regions (10)	**Counties (41)**	**Cities (133)**	**Allocation of Forces**
Grand' Anse	3	12	One Battalion (400)
South	5	18	Three Battalions (1200) / Regional Training Facility-South
North	7	19	One Brigade (1600)/ Regional Training Facility-North
West	5	18	One Division (6400)/ Military Academy
Southeast	3	10	One Battalion (-) (300)
Artibonite	5	15	Two Battalions (800)
Northwest	3	10	One Battalion (400)
Northeast	4	13	One Battalion (400)
Centre	4	12	One Battalion (400)
Nippes	2	6	One Company (100)
Total Security Forces Required 12,000 Soldiers			

Administrative Structure of the Government

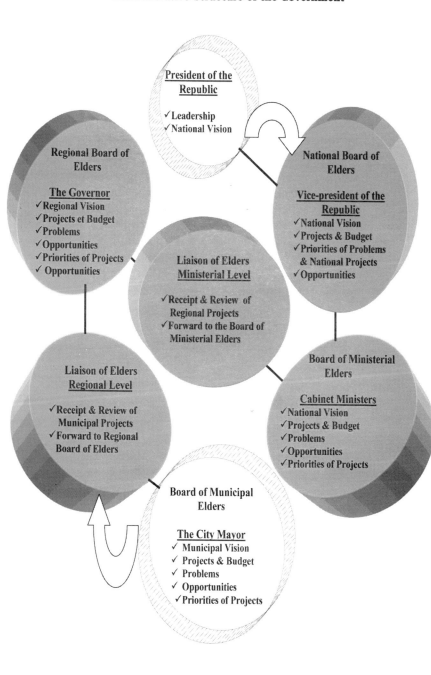

Chapter 7

A Love Letter From God

But the message of the cross is foolishness to those who are perishing, but to us who are being saved, it is the power of God.
1 Corinthians 1:18

For I am not ashamed of the gospel, for it is God's power for salvation to everyone who believes, to the Jew first and also to the Greek. For the righteousness of God is revealed in the gospel from faith to faith, just as it is written, "The righteous shall live by faith."
Romans 1:16-17

The Message of the Cross

Imagine for a moment the Lord Jesus on the cross! See now with your heart the nails the Roman soldiers drove into His hands and feet and the spear that they thrust into His side. These marks remain the eternal seal of His profound love for us. He was beaten all night long, and His body was broken with stripes on His back for our healing. His face was marred unlike any other man. I want to share this message of the cross with you because it is a "love letter" from God that changed my life completely, from a fornicator and a voodoo worshiper to an ambassador of Jesus Christ.

Jesus demonstrated His love for you and me on the cross by paying the full penalty for our sins with His life. Yes - He died for you and me! There is no greater love than to die voluntarily for your enemies. The Bible clearly says that while we were yet helpless, enemies of God, children of wrath and separated from the kingdom of God, Christ died for us. If you ever questioned His love for you, just remember the nail prints in His hands, in His feet. Paul calls this love letter *"The Message of the Cross"* and the Bible calls it *"The Gospel or Good News."*

I write this book especially to tell you that the Lord Jesus Christ loves you. He greatly desires to help you but you must first accept His love and His offer of eternal life. As a child trusts and depends on his parents, Jesus desires to be the source for all of your needs if you would just turn to Him in faith. He wants to fill your hearts with hope. With Him, you can have peace and joy even in the midst of your tribulations. He desires to be a part of your life, to help and comfort you in your time of need. He desires to bless you, establish you in His purpose for your life, and help you to live a fulfilled life.

What Is This Gospel of Which Paul Is Not Ashamed?

It is the great message of God's eternal plan and His unchanging love for humanity. It is the good news of the life, the death, and the resurrection of Jesus Christ. He was bruised and crucified for our transgressions, but God raised Him from the dead for our salvation. This message is a love letter from God to you today! The Apostle John wrote, *"For God so loved the world He gave his only Son, whosoever believe on Him should not perish but have eternal life"* (John 3:16). It is the message of our redemption through Christ Jesus, the Son of God who was perfect (Heb 5:9) and had never sinned. He came to this world and took on Himself the sins of the world and suffered the full penalty. Jesus Christ became the way back to God for you and me. Through His sacrifice, He removes forever the condemnation of our sins and dissolves the obstacles between us and God. We were created to carry out God's plan and to fulfill His purpose on earth. Our sins and iniquities separate us from our Creator. The prophet Isaiah wrote:

"Behold the Lord's hand is not so short that it cannot save; nor His ear so dull that it cannot hear. But your iniquities have made a separation between you and your God, and your sins have hidden His face from you so that He does not hear." (Isaiah 59:1-2)

Many people deny or ignore the existence of God because He will not answer their prayers. The prophet Isaiah tells us that our sins have separated us from God and caused Him not to hear us. The gospel is God's promise of eternal life with Him if we repent of our sins, confess Jesus Christ as our Lord, and believe in our heart that God raised Him from the dead for our salvation. Repentance of sins is deciding to live God's way by turning away from sin and turning to Christ in faith and obedience. The Bible later states that we are reconciled with God and have peace with Him. Then *Isaiah 58:9 says, "Then shall you call, and the Lord shall answer, shall you cry, and He shall say, here I am."*

The Power of the Gospel

Apostle Paul expressed vividly the power of the Gospel in his letter to the Romans: "For I am not ashamed of the gospel, for it is God's power for salvation to everyone who believes, to the Jew first and also to the Greek" (Romans 1:16). I join with this magnificent servant of God in expressing my deepest confidence in the power of the gospel to restore our souls and save us. The Gospel has the power to solve the problems of sin in our lives and to return us to a right standing with God. It is the only way we can be saved from the guilt and power of sin in our lives. The problem of sin must be dealt with seriously because sin has "built-in" judgment and the ultimate penalty is death and eternal separation from God.

The judgment of sin can affect an individual or a nation collectively. Haiti is currently experiencing the ultimate penalty inherent to the sinful behaviors of its people. I shared with you earlier in this book regarding the story of one of my uncles in Haiti who fathered many children by different women. His eldest son followed his sinful path and fathered ten children also by various women without adequate resources to support and educate these children. Thus, primarily the only thing he gave his children was life and nothing more. Like most Haitians, they are small farmers who cultivate the land using primitive means to earn their living. Imagine the inherent consequences for his violations of God's principles on marriage and the impact on his community! This case is not an uncommon lifestyle in Haiti but the accepted norms and practices throughout the nation. The churches and religious leaders are trying, but they lack resources to have a significant impact on national traditions that have been established and practiced for over 200 years.

The message of the cross has not ceased to be the power of God to save, heal, and deliver people from the bondage of sin. Heaven and earth will pass but the word of God shall never pass, because His Word is established in heaven forever. Jesus has not ceased to be our merciful High Priest who moves with compassion for those who are oppressed by the devil. He still desires to walk through our communities, preach in our churches, and lay hands on the sick to heal them. He wants to use us as His instruments if we are available and willing. *2 Chronicles 16:9 states: "The eyes of the LORD search the whole earth in order to strengthen those whose hearts are fully committed to him."*

I spent time reading and reflecting on the book of Acts to see what the first church was teaching and preaching and the results of their efforts. The disciples preached the simple message of the cross and the name of Jesus Christ! It is the same message of the cross Phillip preached at Samaria (Acts 8:6-8). He shared the same love letter you are reading right now. The power of the Gospel proved to be exactly the same when Philip told the people about the life, death, and resurrection of Jesus Christ. As a result, the sick were healed, the blind received sight, devils were cast out, sinners were saved, and Jesus was glorified. The power of the gospel of Jesus Christ was proven the same in Acts 3:6 when Peter told a crippled man: "Silver and gold I do not have, but what I do have I give to you, in the name of Jesus Christ of Nazareth, rise up and walk." The crippled man was made whole. Peter also shared the same love letter from God to the multitudes in Acts 5:14-16 and to Aeneas (Acts 9:34). Faith in the name of Jesus produced great miracles, and Jesus was glorified through Peter's ministry. Paul shared the message of the cross at Lystra in Acts 14:8-10, and the power of the gospel again was proven the same. As Paul preached the gospel, a lame man received faith to be healed while listening to Paul's message.

While I was in Iraq on military service in June 2007, my wife was diagnosed with abnormalities in her breast. The same gospel and power in the name of Jesus healed her. I preached Jesus Christ to one of my brothers who was scheduled to undergo heart surgery in Florida in 2003, he received faith and was perfectly healed. Jesus proved to be the same today for both my brother and my wife. I am happy to share with you this great message of God's mercy, love, and grace—the gospel of Jesus Christ- God's power to save you if you would receive Him in your heart!

Paul says that the righteousness of God is revealed in the gospel from faith to faith. The justice of God declares that we all have sinned and come short of the glory of God (Rom 3:23). There is none righteous—not one! The penalty of sin is death (Rom 6:23), but Jesus died to pay the penalty for our sins (Rom 5:8). This same justice establishes that when you accept Jesus Christ as your personal Savior, God declares you righteous, redeemed, justified, and saved. You become citizens in the Kingdom of God with certain rights, privileges, and authority in the name of Jesus. Without righteousness, fellowship with God is impossible. Having made peace with God, He desires that you know that you can draw near with confidence to the throne of grace (Heb 4:16) - the very presence of God, free from the fear that Adam experienced after he sinned.

The reality is that you are God's best. He loves you and paid in full for all your sins through the suffering of Jesus Christ on the cross. He also provided to you all the spiritual blessings in the heavenly realm through the resurrection of our Lord Jesus Christ. The moment you accept Jesus as your Lord and Savior, your name is officially recorded in heaven as one of God's adopted children. Therefore, I am convinced that the greatest discovery you can ever make is your spiritual identity as a child of God and your position in Christ. God created you in His image and designed you for success and happiness, for life and love, for power and dignity. God expects you to discover your unique value. He created each one of us for a specific purpose. Upon our new birth in Christ, God imparts spiritual gifts in each Christian to enable us to carry out our purpose on earth and to glorify His name. I have learned that God did not create us for shame, despair, or to become a casualty in life. God's greatest desire is for you to discover your unique purpose and how you fit into His plan. It brings me profound joy to discover God's purpose for my life and to be working with Him to actually fulfill His plan for my life.

The Apostle Peter urges us in Acts 2:38 that when we hear the message of the cross and of God's infinite love, we should come to God in repentance, confess our sins to Him, and accept such a great love. Then, God forgives us, receives us, and imparts His power within us, and we become His children and new creatures in Jesus Christ.

As you discover your worth to God and His intense love for you, then you can call on Him in faith and approach His throne of grace with confidence in the name of Jesus, and the miracle you need will be done. I rejoice to know that you have read this book and you have come to realize how much Jesus truly loves you. You don't have to go through the trials of life alone and without the comfort and presence of God within you. Men will betray you, but Jesus can be your trusted friend, your merciful Savior, your light in the dark, your shade in the sun, your rain in dry season, your good doctor when you are sick, your provision in time of need, and your good shepherd who will lead you into green pastures. Most importantly, He wants to be your God, the true source of life who can heal and give rest to your soul. My prayer is that if you do not know Christ in a personal way that you now accept the free gift of eternal life Jesus offers you. I pray that collectively as a nation, we may heed this call to repentance and faith in <u>Jesus Christ, who is the only hope for Haiti</u>. This is the message I am taking to the Haitian people. I am urging you as well to take this great message of God's love to your families and your community.

Endnotes

1. Central Intelligence Agency World Factbook 2008. 30 October 2008 <https://www.cia.gov/ library/ publications/the-world-factbook/geos/ha.html>.

2. Vodou is fully recognized as a religion in Haiti. 5 April 2003 <http://www.hartford-hwp.com/archives/43a/522.html>

3. CIA World Factbook 2008. 30 October 2008 <https://www.cia.gov/library/publications/the-world-factbook/geos/ha.html>.

4. The New Open Bible Study Edition, United of America: The Thomas Nelson, Inc Copyright 1990, p 29.

5. The New Open Bible Study Edition, United of America: The Thomas Nelson, Inc. Copyright 1990, p 669.

About the Author

Before I formed you in the womb I knew you, before you were born I set you apart; I appointed you as a prophet to the nations. (Jeremiah 1:5)

Pierre Rigaud Julien is a native Haitian, born in Chambellan, a small town in the region of Grand' Anse. He immigrated to the United States and later joined the American Army. He served on active duty for 25 years and retired on August 1, 2008 as a Chief Warrant Officer Four (CW4). He served fifteen months in Iraq during Operations Iraqi Freedom in 2006-2008. He participated in Operation Desert Storm and Desert Shield to defend Kuwait during the invasion of Iraq in 1990-1991. He also participated in Operation Just Cause in Panama in 1989 during the arrest of President Manuel Noriega. He is a recipient of many military decorations including the Legion of Merit award for his military service. He became a Christian at age 40. He was ordained and licensed as a minister of the Gospel of Jesus Christ in July 2003. He served as an Evangelist in Belgium from 2003 to 2006. He founded Blessing and Healing Ministries, Inc. in 2004, a non-profit organization, as his vehicle for spreading the Gospel of Jesus Christ to the Haitian people. God entrusted him with the mission of telling the Haitian people to "repent, be baptized, and filled with the Holy Spirit." In this book, Dr. Julien shares what he believes to be the root cause of the socio-economic problems in Haiti and the solution to these problems. Haiti is seriously ill and needs urgent care and a skilled doctor. This book lays before the Haitian people the choices of life or death and urges the nation to choose life and the only source of life — the Lord Jesus Christ.

Jesus is the Answer!

Contact Us:

In the USA:

Blessing & Healing Ministries, Inc.
P.O. BOX 3301
Evans, GA 30809
TEL: (706) 496-2189

In Haiti:

Blessing & Healing Ministries, Inc.
82, Carrefour Shada
Chambellan, Haiti
TEL: (509) 3698-4103

Visit us online:

www.blessinghealing.org
or
Email: admin@blessinghealing.org

Contact us to order additional copies of this book, or to obtain more information about the work of God in Haiti through Dr. Julien's ministry.